MW00353548

CHRISTOPHER W. ANDERSON

I'm not buying it

How to turn today's skeptical Millennials into loyal customers.

Copyright © 2015 by Chris Anderson.

All rights reserved. This book or any portion thereof may not be reproduced or used in any manner whatsoeverwithout the express written permission of the publisher except for the use of brief quotations in a book review.

Printed in the United States of America

First Printing, 2015

ISBN: 978-0-9863494-1-6

Table of Contents

I would like to dedicate this book to my two sons, Cole and Carson, who have given me an insight into the mindset of the next generation and how they communicate, and don't communicate, with people, brands and life. Thanks to my wife Carrie for believing that when I said I needed to get away to write, I was indeed writing.

Foreward

When I go to a seminar and hear a speech, if I walk away with two or three nuggets of wisdom that I believe will help my business, I feel it was time well spent. When I read a book on advertising or marketing, if I glean five or six insights, I feel that book was worth the time it took me to read it.

So, imagine my surprise when I read, "I'm Not Buying It," and realized that this is a treasure load of information, no, actually, almost a roadmap, of how a business can gain insight into the minds, hearts and wallets of a group so many of us have struggled to understand.

The Millennials.

Today, they represent 78 million people in the US. And they are expected to outspend the Baby Boomers by 2018. And, more than any other group, if you win them, they will sell *for* you.

You'll find out exactly what makes them different: the significance of "life points," the critical importance of "scenography," why hiring passionate people is more important than hiring just smart people. And so much more.

Chris Anderson has done his homework. He has shared his first-hand observations in a way that can help any business looking for a way to gain a competitive advantage.

Don't be put off by the fact that Chris has an extensive history in the travel industry and that many of his examples revolve around the restaurant and hotel industry, because this provides a rare look at how Millennials think and act. So many of his examples can be easily translated to any business.

Every once in awhile a marketing book will arrive on my desk that, selfishly, I will devour.

Selfish?

Why?

Because I know from experience that so many competitors will conveniently dismiss or overlook this keen insight and wisdom.

My advice to anyone who wants to succeed in this new world of smartphones, apps and hipsters, is read this book. Then, don't just set it aside and ignore his advice.

Do it.

Thomas J Jordan

Former President, Chairman and Chief Creative Office of HY Connect, an international award-winning communications firm in Chicago and Milwaukee. Tom is author of four best-selling books on marketing and was inducted into the Wisconsin Advertising Hall of Fame in 2014.

My introduction to marketing was a horror show. Literally.

It was 1988 and, at the wise old age of 18, I opened a video store. I was young, energetic, driven – and a little crazy, as most entrepreneurs are.

Still, the move made some sense. Despite my age, I had experience, having managed another video store. The competition was limited, too. At the time, there was no Netflix or Redbox. Not even Blockbuster had moved to my hometown of Lake of the Ozarks, Missouri.

Yet the video store was still a low-margin business and volume was required. I quickly made two observations:

1. I needed more customers coming through the door.

2. When they did, I needed them to rent more than a single movie.

The solution to the two challenges was marketing. Basically, I could market the business or close it. Marketing it was.

I did some advertising in local shoppers and the Yellow Pages to attract more customers. There were a few other such efforts, but most of my time was consumed with the second need: Renting more movies to the customers who were in the store.

Understanding them was
the first step.

There was no Consumer Relationship Management software. I did have some off-the-shelf, video store operating software. It was nothing special – unless you're partial to C:/ prompts.

Still, I turned that alleged software into a database and created customer profiles. I recorded the renters' likes and dislikes, and included the movie preferences of their family members, too.

When my customer Tom came in, all sorts of information about him and his family was at my fingertips. Chances are Tom liked action, while his wife, Betty, preferred drama. Little Billy favored the slasher flicks.

That meant I would have to recommend a movie to Tom. "You'll like this one. Arnold Schwarzenegger is the next Sylvester Stallone." (Remember, it was 1988.)

I also would tell him, "Hey, Betty will like this. Kevin Costner really shows his sensitive side. And here is 'Nightmare on Elm Street Part 91' for Little Billy as well."

The database helped a lot, but it was only half the equation. I also had to find and recommend individual movies that matched their individual preferences.

My recommendations had to be good. If Betty didn't like my selection, Tom wouldn't listen to me next time. The same with Little Billy. Then Tom would leave the store with one movie instead of three, if he came in at all.

That meant I had to watch all the movies to make good recommendations. And I did – about 3,500 to be exact.

Watching the good ones was not a bad day at the office. But the horror flicks were tough; I simply am not a fan.

Still, they had to be watched and analyzed through the prism of, "Would Little Billy like that movie?"

And that's what I did. Looking back, it was a lesson in doing everything possible to deliver customer satisfaction. It was my first glimpse into the premise that you have to know what your customers want – even if you wouldn't want it. You have to put yourself in their shoes.

There were some other lessons, too:

Provide convenience. People want to eat popcorn when they watch their movie. Go to the trouble of providing it. Of course, you might have to ask your customers what they want. Popcorn was a pretty easy guess for me.

Train your employees. Those who worked for me were often on the phone or at the cash register offering advice. They knew the specific questions to ask and recommendations to make. They had to be taught this.

Jobs are on the line. My employees knew we would be out of business if they didn't turn a customer who normally rented a single movie into one who rented three, hopefully with a popcorn and soda kicker. We were all in this together – but they were definitely in it, too. They knew it.

Recommendations matter. I made good ones, so I was a credible source. I also told customers when NOT to rent a movie. That might mean a short-term loss and Tom leaving with two movies instead of three on a particular night. Over the long term, however, I benefitted from the trust gained.

Know where to spread your dollars. When I started the business, I bought an expensive Yellow Pages ad. A week later, a sales rep from Yellow Pages called. Turns out there were quite a few "Yellow Pages." And the one I had paid good money for? Not an important one. Ouch.

People don't mind if products are marketed to them, as long as it's done the right way. Marketing isn't about selling so much as customer service. It's more about providing customers what they want. Deals on popcorn weren't seen as tricky upsells. We were simply providing conveniences.

Marketing can be hard work. Sometimes you have to roll up your sleeves, brace yourself and dive into "Redneck Zombies." Then you have to look at the world through your customers' eyes, which can be challenging.

It would be easy to say, then, that everything I learned 25-plus years ago still applies today. I could even write one of those, "Everything I Needed to Know I Learned In ..." books.

Except it wouldn't be accurate. While there are some tried-and-true lessons and concepts, it's also a different world. Imagine if I were still trying to sell videos using that old C:/ software as a database.

Look how much the video industry has changed since 1988, and the number of players and even business models that have come and gone. It is evidence that all businesses have to change – to adapt to the world around us to survive.

What once was key to attracting, selling and satisfying consumers has changed dramatically. Perhaps most important – the reason I'm focusing on Millennials – is that the new generations are shaping the habits of the world. They possess incredible buying power and it's growing by the day. The Millennials also are driving decisions of those in other generations at an unprecedented level.

Yet it is not the same old marketing models. Millennials need to be handled with care. They need to have the information they want – now – or they'll go somewhere else.

They can spot an ad from a mile away and will run in the opposite direction when they see it. They rely more on genuine, self-generated content from real people they respect.

What about you? Should you stay the same? Change? Both? Neither?

I'll help you figure that out. In this book, I will highlight Millennials' habits and offer solutions to help you connect with them. In fact, each chapter is itself a tip on how, specifically, to market to this group.

Many, but not all, of the real-world examples will reference the travel and hospitality industries. It's not just because that's my world. Those industries are laboratories of human behavior. We spend time studying, reading and assessing our customers more than most other industries. If we fall short – if we don't connect with our customers at a high level – our numbers tumble quickly.

In many ways, I will be making observations as an outsider. I'm not 23 and I don't tweet my friends 24/7. Usually, when I eat at a trendy restaurant, I don't take pictures of my food with my smartphone and post the images on Facebook.

But I get it. I make it my business to get it. Because if I don't get it, I don't get them – the Millennials.

It applies to you, too. The Millennials are going to fuel the success of your business and mine. Or, conversely, they're going to decide whether we run out of gas.

I knew the importance of Millennials before writing this book. Yet during the process of creating it, their significance became even clearer to me.

So did the most important lesson I learned at the video store: Know your customers. Through all the changes over the last few decades, that has remained a constant for successful business.

My goal with this book is to help you know your

Millennial customers – or at least to start
the process.

We have to. Millennials can either deliver
our success or be our horror story. I've
seen enough of the latter to last a lifetime.

CHAPTER ONE
KNOW WHO THEY ARE

The shoe-buying process brought so many elements together you would half expect balloons and streamers to fall as she clicked the "purchase" icon. Wow.

She'll make an impulse buy from time to time, but that's the exception. Usually a lot goes into a purchase, and that certainly was the case with this shoe deal.

She first heard about TOMS shoes from a friend's Facebook posting. She learned that TOMS gives a pair of shoes to underprivileged children every time a customer buys a pair for themselves. Pretty cool.

She used her phone to visit the TOMS site. (When is the last time she used that phone to talk? On Mother's Day?) The photos of adorable kids won her over. She downloaded the TOMS app and promised herself she would come back later and buy some shoes. She did, but not until she had followed the company for a while.

Maybe you've seen her. Maybe she comes through the doors of your business or the portal of your website on a regular basis.

Or ... maybe you haven't seen her.

Maybe you confused "courting" with stalking and creeped her out.

Maybe you just don't have the value. That hurts, because it's not that you're expensive; she'll pay a higher price for what she deems a superior product.

Of course money isn't everything. Maybe you didn't

make her feel good about herself. (The shoe giveaway sure does.)

She might have made it to your website, but didn't feel a connection when she arrived. (Those underprivileged kids on the TOMS website – well, you already heard they were adorable. Their photos were shot by a pro, too. The connection she felt was no coincidence.)

It could be that you didn't set the scene. Yes, set the scene. She likes that.

She's very demanding. You might even say a bit of a diva.

But here's the deal: She represents a group that by 2020 will spend $1.7 trillion annually. They will account for 30 percent of the retail spending in the U.S.

That's a tough number to overlook. It seems you have

two options: Figure out how to reach her, or find a new line of work.

I hear TOMS shoes is hiring.
Who is "she"?
A Millennial, of course.

Millennials are men and women born between 1977 and 1992. (There are many age variations, but those are the numbers I'm using.) They can be a tough crowd, to be sure.

They are picky, fickle, finicky and downright skeptical. They live in a world of fine lines. As referenced, they want to be "courted" but not "stalked." Pay attention to me, but not too much attention.

That's just their attitude. Connecting gets even tougher if you factor in some of their habits, unheard of only a generation ago. Millennials infrequently watch television ON a television, and they treat their phone as if it's some kind of central command.

So shake your head, roll your eyes, mumble about the good old days. Then think about that $1.7 trillion.

That's quite a number, and it's getting bigger because the rest of us are picking up Millennials' quirky habits – making their reach even stronger. (You like your phone plenty, too. And you watched season four of "Breaking Bad" during a single weekend.)

There is some good news.

ONE. We know Millennials can be a tough crowd. Half of the solution is understanding the challenge, right?

TWO. There are approaches that can help you connect with them.

THREE. I will share those tactics in this book.

Who exactly are these guys?

Before that, I want to share some numbers and observations to further define the Millennial.

They're big. With 78 million Millennials in the U.S., they comprise the largest segment of the population. They differ from both the Gen Xer (born between 1965 and 1980) and the Baby Boomer (born 1946-1964) in almost
every way. The Millennial generation is a goal oriented, tech-savvy, optimistic, self-confident, constantly-connected group of independent thinkers.

They are often broken into two groups. As of 2015, they will be 23 years old on the young end, and 38 on the other. There can be a lot of differences based on life stages, though many themes still resonate with all ages. It's more of a mindset than an age group.

They spend. They are predicted to surpass the spending power of the boomers by as early as 2018. As noted earlier, they are expected to spend $1.7 trillion annually in the U.S. by 2020.

They care. While focused on the "me," Millennials also are very globally aware and interested in brands and companies that support causes they feel are important.

They have seen some things. They aren't connected by dates of birth as much as shared experiences. First, they've grown up during massive changes in technology. They witnessed the worst terror attack ever to take place on U.S. soil. They were shaken by the 2008 financial crisis, and some of them are leaving higher education to enter into the worst job market in three generations.

They enjoy spending. Nearly 60 percent say they "love to shop," an increase of almost 20 percent when compared to Gen Xers.

They love "life points." Millennials love to travel, buy apparel and dine out – even when their budget does not justify it. These enjoyable activities are considered "life points." They are 65 percent more likely to dine out with friends and colleagues than are other age groups.

They are not loyal. They are not loyal to a job or companies in general. Most expect to work for their current employer for only three years, and many have already switched careers at least once.

Except when they are loyal. They are very loyal to brands they believe in. Most associate themselves with brands that have a history or story that is aligned with their beliefs. When they select a brand, they will generally stick with it and be "off the market" for competitors.

Suitors can come a-calling. They also love to be "courted" by brands. Notice I did not say "sold," as this turns them off. They feel brands should entertain them as part of the courting process. Millennials believe it is important for brands and businesses to make them smile.

But … no stalking please. Millennials in focus groups have said they will not buy from a company that tracks their online activities and then targets advertising at them. Millennials see this as stalking and not selling. (The ads might even prove counterproductive because Millennials might speak negatively about the brand to others.)

It's OK for them to watch you. This same group will follow their loyal brands on their social networks and "like" some promotions or enable push notifications. (When considered with the stalking point above, yet another fine line the marketer must walk.)

They will sell for you. This group will promote its favorite products and services through social media. Millennials can watch a "Transformers 4" movie trailer a half dozen times and not take action, yet head to the theater if a friend makes a recommendation via text, Twitter or Facebook.

Value means a lot. Similar to Gen Xers and Boomers, Millennials are very focused on getting a great value for their money. They believe having a positive and interactive experience with a brand in a retail environment is a must and say that this weighs heavily on their decision to purchase and return in the future.

Cheap is not better. "Value" does not mean cheap, and it does not mean "clearance rack." Value is a product they like at a decent price. They are more willing than the two previous generations to spend additional money for products or services they "deem" worth the extra costs.

They are truly a social generation. They rely on authentic, user-generated content to make decisions more soundly. When buying electronics, cars, hotels, insurance or any major purchase, they rely on the testimonials and ratings provided by others.

Who do you trust? They are more likely to trust the opinion of a stranger or random anonymous social groups than any stats or ratings the brands provide.

Impulse buyers. They will make impulse buys if the purchase makes them feel good, even if they don't have the money.

Smartphones do the heavy lifting. They believe the phone is the most important tech device they own, even though most also have laptops and tablets. The smartphone is mostly used for texting and the apps, while the phone function itself doesn't get used nearly as much. Almost half of this group has made a purchase using their smartphones.

Going mobile. Almost two-thirds of all mobile shoppers come from this generation. This group researches products and services online, often immediately before taking action. Millennials are heavily influenced by apps that can assist in the shopping and decision-making process.

Nowhere to hide. Because they are so often connected, we know where to find them. Not surprisingly this group is very active in social media, with 80 percent on Facebook, 50 percent on LinkedIn, 30 percent on Twitter, 23 percent on YouTube and Google, and 20 percent on Pinterest and Instagram.

Ready for action. They describe themselves to others as happy, fun, sociable, confident, curious, healthy, fit and looking to become healthier and improve their appearance. (Sounds like they are in the market for just about everything.)

A purchase that says something. A substantial number of Millennials (42 percent) say that buying something that makes them feel good about themselves is "very important," and 88 percent think it is "very or somewhat important." In addition, most say that buying something that will make them stand out is also very important.

Seeing is believing. Their web-savvy nature means they are more likely to appreciate sophisticated content. Great visuals are a must and keep them targeted in a lifestyle with the user in mind.

The "mirror effect." Millennials like to imagine themselves in the scene or using the products that are represented.

Multi-taskers. This group has the greatest propensity and volition to "multi-screen," or use different types of technology at the same time.

On their schedule. They expect content whenever and wherever they want it. About 40 percent would rather stream programs over the Internet than adjust their schedule to fit the broadcasters' schedule. Millennials are creating a phenomenon of time-shifting – watching programs in a grouping of recordings instead of the live broadcast on television.

For the Millennial, it is an al a carte world.

What does it mean to you?

Negotiating some fine lines and likely working a little harder. A little creativity can make a difference, too.

The bottom line is they are consumers – and they are on pace to consume a lot. They will buy, which is obviously very good news. You just need to make that connection to make sure they buy from you.

CHAPTER TWO

HELP THEM CROSS THE
APPREHENSION THRESHOLD

Sometimes you find a reward in this business that you didn't expect. I had that happen to me a few months back at the Grand Geneva Resort & Spa.

It's a pretty darn nice place. It's also a family-friendly place, particularly on weekends when specific packages cater to that group. The weekend getaway provides a chance for the family unit to reconnect, and for the parents to re-engage each other, too. The weekends can be very therapeutic, particularly considering the scenic, natural setting in Lake Geneva, Wis.

On that particular day – a Friday – I was in the lobby when in walked a woman. She moved fast and did not smile. She seemed to be carrying the weight of the world, though all she had in her hand was a piece of paper.

Behind her came a husband and two children, ages 8 and 10 or thereabouts. There was a shortage of smiles, to say the least.

I had a pretty good idea what had happened.

The woman had been excited when she booked the reservation a week ago. She had said, "Forget the budget. We have to get away." Maybe her family didn't see much of one another. Maybe someone was having trouble at school, or work wasn't going well.

At the time it seemed like a good idea. Since booking the reservation, however, doubts had crept in – and they had grown stronger during the drive. Most of Grand Geneva's guests come from an hour or so away. Maybe the kids were acting up in the car; maybe the husband had questioned how good this weekend was going to be after all.

Based on the way she clutched that receipt, she had the same questions in mind as she came in the door. She had booked the room – for leisure travel, 88 percent of the time the woman of the house does – and now she regretted it.

In fact, walking into the hotel had probably been the lowest point of her day, maybe even her week. She had tried to do something for the good of the family, and what does she get? Screaming kids and a second-guessing husband?

Right there, as she walked in, I smiled. Not because I enjoy seeing guests in misery. I smiled because I knew her luck was about to change.

The hotel's ambassador has seen guests like this before—many of them. He immediately approached the woman, welcomed her and then welcomed the children.

He had gifts for the kids, too. Yes, he was glad they were there. They were welcome!

The woman almost smiled. It was a start.

Then the ambassador provided a schedule of children's activities for that weekend. Now the woman was even more certain the children were welcome. She and her husband might even find some time to reignite their relationship, too.

In less than a minute, everything had changed. The kids were happy, the father was happy – he even let go of the children's wrists – and the woman smiled.

That smile was no accident. The events that had put her at ease was part of the scenography at that hotel.

Scenography is important. It's creating a scene – an environment – for memorable experiences.

I call this "scenography" because in the theater a scenographer is a person who integrates all elements of the play – the scenery, the props, the lighting, the costumes,the script and the actors' movements – to create an outstanding production for the audience.

At the Grand Geneva, the ambassador was just one part of the scenography, which is discussed in detail in the next chapter.

But one particular aspect of scenography, crossing the apprehension threshold, is crucial because it is the opening act for any business. It is the impression we make on customers, and it can be hard to recover from the wrong start. It also warrants extra discussion in regards to reaching Millennials.

Millennials are about experiences. They are typically willing to pay a premium price but they expect a premium experience in return. In other words, they expect value.

You'll have to provide that value the minute they walk in the door, or they might not return. (Or maybe they'll just turn around and leave, based on what kind of business you're in.)

Millennials communicate about their experiences. If the woman had a bad weekend, her friends on social media would find out–and so would their friends. When the opposite happened, her friends are more likely to become guests, too.

This family is likely to become return guests. Retaining business is a cornerstone of virtually every plan.

* * *

The apprehension threshold is something every consumer faces, whether in person or online.

I've experienced, it too. In fact, I started taking a closer look at our lobbies after immersing myself in the Harley-Davidson brand.

HD was one of our largest customers in Milwaukee, and I needed to understand their brand to be the best partner. That meant going through a four-day riding course, earning my license and renting a bike. It also meant visiting Harley-Davidson dealerships.

I've been in hundreds of hotels, and was so accustomed to entering them that I admittedly had lost some perspective regarding the apprehension a person can feel when entering a business.

That feeling was certainly with me as I entered the Harley-Davidson dealership. My visit occurred after work and I wore a suit, not typical Harley attire. It was a Friday so I thought there might be parties going on at the dealership. I envisioned a bunch of bikers having fun while a guy in a suit walks in. Not the end of the world – I'm a big boy – but something to think about.

In the parking lot, my heart started racing when I left the car. I forged ahead, walked into the store and was greeted by … nothing.

No parts department desk, no sales office, no greeter. They let me walk in and wander around and spend a few minutes looking at bikes and whatever else I chose to check out.

It took 15 minutes for an employee to approach me. Now, to be perfectly clear this was not poor customer service – just the opposite. They were letting me become comfortable and realized the best way to do that was to not approach me and be perceived as pressuring. (I was later told the dealers don't want to be viewed as pushy "used car" types.)

A staff member eventually walked my way. He explained the layout of the store, and said he was here to help; give him a shout if I had a question. He most certainly did not ask what he needed to do to put me in metal that day.

In fact, during a conversation (that I initiated) a few minutes later, he told me they wouldn't put me in metal for months. It takes the average HD customer 11 months, from the day they walk into a store until the day they buy a bike. Speeding up that process increases the likelihood of a return, I was told. "If people make impulse buys, they bring the bike back," the staffer told me.

He did provide information on riding courses,
licensing and bikes when asked.

As I looked around other comforts appeared. Soft
clothing was mixed with the metal to create a gentler
look. Lighting was soft, too. The smell of leather,
another comfort to our senses, filled the store.

I felt comfortable and, yes, I went back.

What makes customers apprehensive when visiting
your business or even your website? Could a fresh
look at your business lead to ideas that would help
remove that apprehension?

There are ways Marcus Hotels & Resorts tries to
lessen the apprehension threshold. These same
lessons would apply to most other businesses.

No staring, please. Guests don't want to feel like they're on stage when they enter. Whenever possible, hotel desks are to the side and do not face the door. Lobby furniture for other guests usually doesn't face the door either.

Greetings. If there is a line at the desk, we make sure an ambassador greets the waiting guests and makes them feel welcome.

Treat them all the same. The woman at the Grand Geneva was an older Millennial. But don't forget younger Millennials. They are in their early 20s and often feel out of place at a "nicer" establishment. Make them feel comfortable, even if they might not be dressed differently. Put them at ease in a world that often judges them and you'll have a loyal customer.

Make it quick. The check-in process should be a quick turnaround. However, we also try to gather valuable information so we find the right room fit, which is in fact another source of apprehension in our business. Are you asking your customers the right questions when they walk in your "door"?

Keep customers in the dark. People tend to move to darker spaces. It's part of our DNA. That's why we use softer Edison bulbs to light our facilities. This is important at bars and restaurants, too. LED lights are too bright and basically ruin moments. (There are some improvements in LED lights, but they haven't gone far enough for me.)

Limit the use of overhead lights. Your customers will never be comfortable in lighting that is better suited for an autopsy. Instead, use task lighting (lighting placed for a specific purpose) when it makes sense, for example, to light up a desk. The key is to illuminate a particular area, instead of shining a bright light on everything. Highlight what you want them to see.

Be fire inspired. Humans find the flickering light of a fireplace comforting. I believe that goes back to our time in the womb, when certain objects are illuminated through our mother's skin. Those flickering images – whether from a fireplace, candle or even LED candle – provide comfort.

Natural colors comfort. Sunset colors and those associated with the sun are soothing. Use them.

By the book. Books provide comfort in several ways and have been essential design elements since Gutenberg.

First, they remind us of calm, safe places where we feel welcome. (Have you ever been run out of a library?) Put books on display, but not all in a perfect row. Make their presence look unstaged, like a den or library at home.

Books also have a particular scent. If you buy antique books and put them in the lobby (or whatever your "lobby" is), your customers will smell them when they walk in, and the comfort will be there, too.

Music matters. Heart rates increase anytime there is not music. Most every selling environment includes music. It is another key to removing the apprehension threshold. Make sure customers can hear it when they enter.

If you don't think music matters, think about where it isn't played. The two places I can think of are the DMV and the post office. Not exactly anxiety-free locations.

The point is that details matter. They determine how your business is perceived. A customer won't walk in and say, "I am catching the slight aroma of a book." But he will take in the whole scene and draw conclusions about whether he feels welcome. Once established, that perception can be difficult to change.

E-anxiety

There is an electronic threshold, too – your website. You need to set the scene there as well. Remember, Millennials often research before they buy and sometimes simply go ahead and make the purchase online.

You need to help them feel welcome and comfortable on your website, too. How?

Use Responsive Web Design. With RWD, the site determines what device is accessing it and adjusts accordingly. It enables great viewing, easy reading and trouble-free navigation whether on a laptop or smartphone. This tends to be more of an issue for smaller businesses, but some corporations have problems as well. They might have a larger corporate site with RWD, but individual sites – for franchises, for example – have not been updated.

Use quality images. Millennials tend to stay on sites and ultimately complete a transaction if it has good photography and layout.

Be intuitive. Your site can't be tough to navigate. Frustrated Millennials leave – and take their business with them – likely for good.

Tell them your good side. Millennials are a socially conscious group that leans toward socially conscious businesses. If your company supports a cause, say so on your site. The same rule applies to your use of local resources. Millennials like that. If you do it, tell them.

Let them follow you. Again, Millennials don't like to be stalked, but they do often follow organizations they like and might want to do business with. Prominently post a way for them to follow you.

CHAPTER THREE

SET THE SCENE

One hotel I visited thought so far outside the box that they put someone inside the box.

True story. Here I was talking to the desk clerk while checking into a hotel in Los Angeles. Movement caught my eye and I did a double take.

Sure enough, behind the desk was a huge aquarium. It had no fish or exotic reptiles, but a woman. She just sat down reading a book, and, I later noticed, took a nap. I suppose reading in an aquarium all day can wear you out.

The woman in the aquarium absolutely fascinated me – and other guests, too. She was the talk of the lobby, and her presence put everyone at ease. There also were photos and social media postings. It was a clear "Wow!"

You better believe I discussed this back at the office. I often explain the value of "unexpected treats" to my team. (Well, I explain it a lot, so maybe "preach" is a more accurate term than "explain.")

The unexpected treat is exactly what it sounds like: finding something you didn't expect – something positive. If done right, the unexpected treat can be a real differentiator. We need them in the hospitality industry, and you need them in your business, too.

Now, putting a human in an aquarium might not be the treat you choose. I never considered it for our hotels, either. But we need to stand out and create a "wow" factor for our guests and customers in ways that don't require extensive use of glass cleaner. Or conflicts with it.

We have opportunities to do this at various scenes in our businesses. When we put these scenes together, we have "scenography." Not every scene will be a "wow," but together they should keep customers on a path to create memories. That is the ultimate goal.

In the last chapter, we talked about threshold apprehension, and how we need to help our customers overcome anxieties when they first walk in the door. There are other scenes, too, and customers can be won and lost at these stages.

We have to make sure they aren't lost, and we do this by creating scenes. If we get a "wow" in there once in a while, all the better. We're then that much closer to the experience.

What is scenography?

When someone asks me to define scenography, I always say, "It's what you do before a couple arrives at your house for dinner."

During the hour before their arrival, you turn on the outside lights. You light candles and maybe the fireplace.

The cooking is under way, which creates a great aroma. The wine glasses are wiped clean, and the bottle uncorked. Music is playing.

That's scenography.

What about the execution at your day job? How do you actually do this? Here's the formula, "Empathetic Observations + Strategic Design Thinking = EXPERIENCE INNOVATION."

Empathetic observations

Let's break that equation down. Empathy means putting yourself in someone else's shoes. Take a walk around your business and look at it with fresh eyes.

If you were a customer, what would you think at this spot, and that place, and this point? What jumps out, and what looks bland? Do you have an underutilized asset – for example, a great view but nowhere to sit and watch it? A great house band with poor acoustics? Great clothes in your boutique but racks so crowded they're essentially an eyesore?

Walking around your business is a start, but you will need a second opinion. Real estate agents increasingly use stagers before listing a home. Stagers are outsiders who tour a soon-to-be-listed home and say, "This place is more likely to sell quickly, and at a higher price, if you make these improvements."

Often the homeowner is stunned at the suggestions. Sometimes they just don't realize that their home is dated or unappealing in certain ways. Often they're told about trouble spots that they knew were there but became desensitized to over time.

Your business might have these, too. Have an outsider take a walk and tell you what he sees.

Strategic design thinking

Most large companies hire professional designers, and some even employ one in-house. Smaller firms should hire a designer, with very few (and maybe not any) exceptions. Why? Because any design work that you might be able to do by yourself will look like you did it … yourself.

Spend some money and use the updates as an opportunity to re-introduce your business and brand. Throw a party, have an open house, tell the world you've improved your scenography. Only use a catchier phrase.

Experience innovation

Remember, the equation ended with "experience innovation." That's the ultimate goal – not necessarily to stop at the "wow," but to have it be part of an overall amazing, memorable experience. "Wow" scenes help with that experience, but so do, say, wine tastings in your bar or scheduled services for the children. Or special coffee in your suite.

Other pieces to the puzzle

The equation covers several core concepts, but there are other considerations as well. We also say scenography is:

- **Staged.** Essentially, staging is a powerful yet organic way to control an experience. We lead guests to the right path, but we do not tell them what to do – or which direction to take. Don't forget: Millennials prefer self-discovery. If you talk at them, they won't listen.

- **An initiative.** We plan memorable experiences for our guests. We can't count on these acts happening randomly. We expedite the experience.

Beyond empathy

Walking in someone else's shoes is part of the discovery. You also should learn from other processes.

Focus on individuals in natural contexts. Watch your customers. Where do they go? What do they do? Where do they pause and take a look? What do they walk past without so much as a second thought?

Uncover latent needs. Customers might not be able to tell you what they want, because they might not know what it is. Figure it out for them. Watch them, as referenced in the previous point, and keep records or journals of observations. Then spot trends over time.

Look at your documentation. What suggestions have customers made? What have they complained about?

A walk through the entire process

I would like to walk you through the scenography process. I hope you can apply all or parts of it to your business as well.

We implement scenography in five steps that DASIL (pronounced "dazzle"). This mnemonic will remind you to:

1. Define the theme
2. Align the theme
3. Select stages
4. Implement scenes
5. Live it

ONE. Define the Theme

The theme is the "big idea" that ties the guest experience together. To help define it, we consider:

Brand relevance. Does the theme emphasize the "lifestyle" part of our brand? Is it consistent with what we do?

Competitive considerations. What are interesting trends in the industry – and beyond? Are others finding success with certain themes? Can we borrow and improve some of those ideas?

Guest experience impact. What do guests find memorable about the property?

TWO. Align the Theme

Once you've developed a theme, all the elements of a property should align with it. We ensure that's the case by examining (or auditing) three key areas:

Props. For us, that's furniture, food and beverage, letters and documents, in-room amenities, flower arrangements, glassware and china, and decorative elements.

Tone. That includes service language, service behaviors, uniforms and messages/communications to guests.

Mood. The mood is set through fragrances and aromas, lighting, acoustics and style of music.

THREE. Select Stages

When all guest aspects are aligned with the theme, consider which stages best bring the theme to life.

This is where you need to be aware of your customers' movements and flow, and possible opportunities to set scenes along the way. We do this by creating a collection of stages or scenes. We develop a grid of key points at our properties: the lobby,
transitions (immediately after check-in and at departure), the guest room, the spa, our retail facilities, the restaurant, the club level and the exterior.

FOUR. Implement Scenes

This is where we consider and integrate all factors that contribute to a seamless guest experience. What specifically does that mean? Following are some ways we implemented scenes at our key points.

Lobby. An immediate welcome. A quick check-in for our guests and makes them feel like VIPs, and that we knew they were coming. When possible, a counterless check-in also removes a barrier between us and our customers.

Transitions. Guests who wait in the lobby for friends or business companions can observe art, with content available if they would like to learn, and historical information that ties into the theme.

Also regarding transition, we provide a parting gift to guests. They feel like they've been treated well throughout their stay and then – just when they thought the experience was over – we present a surprise send-off.

Guest room. We have a "seize the day" scene where we leave a personal note about an experience available in the hotel that guests might like to try (wine tastings, live music for example).

Retail. We offer many of the products we use at the hotel – at the bar, restaurants and even in the rooms – in retail shops. Guests like to experience new products, such as that cool coffee maker in the room. We offer the convenience of having them available for purchase.

Restaurant. We offer "A Big Night In" and create an environment as rich as anything available outside our building.

Club Level. This special access area features local spirits with information for those who want to learn more. The exclusivity and local products provide an unforgettable experience.

The Exterior. The facility is tidy, of course, but also offers places for guests to pause and take in a particularly picturesque view. Outdoor gardens and/ or sculptures (with information available for those who want it) often tie into the local culture.

FIVE. **Live It**

Bring all these elements together – bring them to life – and create a living, enduring brand. That means putting the pieces together and also making sure they are properly nourished once created.

Scenography is a lot of time and effort, but it ultimately creates experiences, which Millennials demand. Create the experience and you'll connect with them. How far outside the box you go to accomplish this is up to you.

Making it Millennial

Remember that your scenes need features that connect with Millennials.

Self-discovery. Millennials like to learn on their own. Have information available, but don't push it.

Be genuine. Millennials like real materials – real wood and real bricks. Take shortcuts, and your scene setting will not meet their standards.

Keep it local. Millennials appreciate local food sources and local culture.

Customer service. Millennials like to be courted and treated well. They sometimes feel slighted, particularly younger Millennials. Proper customer service at every scene is crucial.

CHAPTER FOUR
RAISE YOUR CUSTOMER
SERVICE BAR

I won't bore you by starting this chapter with a customer service nightmare story. You've no doubt had your own – maybe as recently as this morning when you bought a cup of coffee, a few hours later when you visited a business at lunch or during a stop on your way home from work.

In fact, there's a chance you had an issue at every one of those places.

The bar is set very low for customer service these days, and somehow businesses still manage to under-deliver – even when the expectation is mediocrity. Amazing.

Customer service tips usually center around such clichés as, "The customer is always right," which of course is and isn't true. Sometimes managers try to instill friendliness into a staff with observations such as, "It takes more muscles to frown than smile."

The good news is you won't be reading that crap here. What I do want to share are less obvious customer service efforts, and why and how they matter to Millennials. If you're looking for the standard practices – which your business most certainly should be aware of and adhere to – there are many other places to go.

Why customer service matters to Millennials

Why devote a specific chapter to customer service in a book about Millennials?

They are a slighted generation. They arrive at businesses expecting to be treated poorly, in part because of how they often dress, which is sometimes not all that nice. When the inevitable happens, it bothers them. They're sort of looking for trouble.

They will tell the whole world. If they find the trouble, they'll get out that beloved smartphone and rip you apart in platforms that distribute far, deep and wide. If you keep your promise – or, heaven forbid, over-deliver – they'll talk about that, too.

They are loyal. If you win them over, they'll bring you their return business.

A few tips to keep them happy

You're committed to reaching Millennials, and, of course, you would like to do some business with them, too. What steps can you take to make sure you don't knock the chip off their shoulder, and they don't tell the rest of the world that you did?

ONE. Answer their question with a question.

Doing so helps hone in on what they want. (You'll find "what they want" will be local, authentic and many other such topics that are discussed in detail in other parts of this book.)

The catch here is that if you don't ask questions, and then give them the wrong information, you will, in fact, knock that chip off their shoulder.

Remember that these people are about the experience. If you don't have specifics, you'll give them bad advice, and their experience will not meet their expectations.

And ... they'll blame you.

In hotels, we are on the front line of the follow-up question issue. Many times daily our staff is asked, "Do you know a good restaurant?" We have to ask questions to find out the type of food our customers like, whether they want to walk to the restaurant, their price threshold, the general atmosphere they prefer, and other pieces of information.

We uncover this information by asking. Also, as these questions are asked, we keep in mind that Millennials typically want an experience. (Sorry, Applebee's.)

So, I suggest you get all the facts before offering the advice (in the case of a hotel) or attempting to connect them with a specific product or service (many other businesses).

TWO. Hire the right people.

Obvious, yes, but I have a trick here: Hire based on attitude, not appearance. Choose attitude over skill . . . attitude over knowledge.

My theory is parents shape attitudes at an earlier age, and for a much longer period, than any employer will ever be able to undo. That means the new hire needs the proper outlook on day one; you and I can't fix them on the attitude front.

What's my trick? I'll often hire someone with a good attitude – and no knowledge – and train them.

We absolutely must have a good attitude at hotels. It's one of our key differentiators. Housekeeping, maintenance, the food and beverage team, the concierge and front desk people – they all have to be "people people."

Yet attitude applies to retail and other industries as well. Surprisingly, these sectors don't always realize this, at least not when hiring. They'll employ a well-dressed introvert who hates talking to people, and their businesses will suffer.

I would say "hire for attitude" was stating the obvious if I didn't encounter bad attitudes so frequently.

THREE. Hire passionate people.

There is a saying in the restaurant business: Never trust a skinny chef. I think that goes back to passion.

The overweight chef probably loves to eat, though I suppose he could have some medical issue or glandular disorder. (In this book, let's assume the extra pounds result from eating.)

When I go to a steakhouse, I want a waiter who's on the heavy side, and I want him to come out and tell me I absolutely must have a particular cut of ribeye. I want him to care if I get that steak.

During our hiring process, I ask people about their passions. The other day, I heard the perfect answer from a man applying to be a restaurant manager.

"What do you want to be when you grow up?" I asked, a question that gives the candidate a chance to talk about his passion.

"I want to own a ranch," he said. He went on to explain that he would love to till the land and grow his own vegetables. He would want chickens and some livestock, too. He was sort of the sustenance type.

Fantastic! He wants to learn everything about growing, raising, cooking and serving food – a passion that is a great fit for a restaurant manager. He was hired.

FOUR. Don't put layers between

you and the customers.

A wise boss repeated the above statement over and over to me. Now it's just ingrained.

In fact, I'll do almost anything I can to tear those barriers down – even if it can't be accomplished through physical means.

I was involved with managing the Atlanta Marriott Marquis. It's a fascinating place with a fascinating history. When it was built in 1985, its breathtaking 47-story atrium was the world's largest. At 470 feet tall, the atrium could fit the Statue of Liberty atop her pedestal – with more than 100 feet to spare.

It's interesting to watch guests enter the hotel for the first time. They walk in and their jaws drop as they take in the vastness.

And then ...

And then they look back down to Earth, and their expression goes from amazed to confused and bewildered as their eyes settle on the longest front desk in the history of mankind. The hotel makes the world's best first impression, and the world's worst second impression.

The desk held 15 check-in terminals. The guests have to walk toward the desk, and the layout is such that everyone in the hotel faces the newcomer, who feels the eyes on him or her, like asking for a loan.

Getting rid of the desk was not an option. An expensive rehabilitation had taken place shortly before my arrival, and trying to get the new football-field-length desk removed would have been all but impossible. It was a battle not worth fighting.

Instead, we put someone on the customers' side of the desk to help transition the guests from the initial awe to the daunting check-in.

We utilized friendly, outgoing employees and placed one per shift at a strategic spot in front of the desks. He or she always wore bright red and became the ambassador.

That ambassador greeted the guests as they took in the atrium (before the second impression had a chance to occur) and said, "Isn't this magnificent?

The hotel is 1,675 rooms. The Christo is an original art piece. In fact, it's the largest piece of hanging art in the world."

Conversation also centered on John Portman, Jr., who designed the building. "Mr. Portman still lives next door," remarked the ambassador. Eventually, the conversation led the ambassador to ask, "Can I take your bag and get you checked in?"

The ambassador walked the guest to the desk, said, "It was nice to meet you. Julie here will take care of you. If there's anything else you ever need from me, let me know. And if you're up there," pointing to the atrium, "you can always see me right here."

That was the transition: A little conversation, a reminder that the guest always has quick access to help despite the vastness of the atrium and the desk.

Many retailers make their own transition mistake. They might make a good impression, but don't have a customer service ambassador to help someone transition into the store. That can be the difference between a great experience (and sales) or an early exit.

FIVE. Be deep, not wide.

The ultimate proof that customer service matters is Ace Hardware. This fits Millennials in particular because they are the "self-discovery" generation, so they are more inclined to take on a project and figure it out as they go along. When they get lost, they'll need some help.

Ace has withstood the heavy blows from Home Depot and Lowe's. They've done so by their second-to-none customer service.

Walk into an Ace Hardware and you'll be greeted by someone with knowledge – someone who can help you finish the project you're in the middle of (and maybe in the middle of screwing up).

There is no greeting from some of the big box stores, and the response to a question is often along the lines of, "If we have it, it's in aisle 93."

Not at Ace. An Ace employee often greets the customer at the door to see if help is needed. Another employee is typically located near the back, for those who earlier turned away help but now realize they need it.

Ace's game plan is to stay focused on, and stay close to, the customer. The business doesn't have superior products, and the stores aren't the fanciest. Yet they have survived because they have knowledge.

Ace employees also don't typically make you feel like a fool for asking a question. Their knowledge is deep, and they share it. They don't knock the chip off the Millennial shoulder.

SIX. Empower your employees.

Your employees are on the front line, dealing with the customer. They need to be able to make decisions and not be second-guessed when they do. That includes decisions with a financial impact.

Authorize them to provide a freebie to a customer or reduce the cost of a service. Let them know that problem resolution is theirs to handle as they see fit.

When they do make a decision, praise them. Don't go back and second-guess lost dollars.

We have had hotel general managers jump in cars and rush to the airport to deliver an item that a guest left behind. It's time-consuming and sometimes a bit over-the-top if the item isn't essential, but it shows we value the guest's business and will do whatever we can to earn his loyalty.

At Marcus, those efforts are rewarded, not scrutinized. We're convinced the costs are more than covered in business gained.

SEVEN. Follow up.

One common mistake is to put a customer service process in place, and then assume it continues.

It often doesn't. Check back in. Follow up with employees to ensure they're still focusing on the customer.

$$* * *$$

Think about the last time you had a poor customer service experience. It no doubt could have been easily avoided.

Then consider how many more such experiences you would have if you entered the situation with a Millennial-sized chip on your shoulder.

CHAPTER FIVE
FIND A SOCIAL CAUSE

The sun was shining and the music was flowing as I drove to work that day. A DJ came on the air and gave me a little information on the song I had just heard. She sounded very "Millennialish": a little angsty, upbeat, cynical – the whole deal wrapped into one.

Then she said, "Did you hear about the Starbucks deal?" I had not, but she was about to tell me.

Starbucks, which she "usually avoids" because she prefers "local places" had released news the previous day that impressed her. Starbucks had struck a deal with a university to offer online classes, and ultimately diplomas, to employees who had not finished school.

It turns out many Starbucks employees have devoted some time to college, but haven't finished. The company was aware of this, so they offered to pick up the tab for those employees who wanted to graduate.

Starbucks shared this good news with the rest of the world, and the message resonated with the DJ. "Maybe I'll have to go to Starbucks once in a while after all," she said.

This was so on-target for the Millennial mindset that it seemed scripted. I had done some writing on this book the previous night, and not 12 hours later, a Millennial was on the radio behaving like someone straight out of central casting.

A few points struck me.

1. This stuff really does work. Social causes do connect with this group.

2. Millennials will spread the word about a company's involvement in social causes. A DJ might be an extreme example, but everyone's voice is a little louder with today's communication platforms.

3. Millennials will try your brand if you make the connection. The DJ said she would.

4. You can create the social cause. Whatever Starbucks' motivation – self-promotion, a genuine desire to help employees or a combination of both – it came up with the social connection. It manufactured

it, built it. You don't have to be an organic farmer or a recycling business to find social causes that connect with Millennials. You can develop your own.

Some less traditional social causes

Of course, the coffeehouse is ripe for the social cause crowd. Starbucks has a "responsibility" section on its website that explains how it contributes to the greater good on many fronts.

But what if your business doesn't serve four types of granola? No problem. There are connections to be made in virtually any industry.

Case Construction Equipment is a great example.

Case builds construction equipment of all shapes and sizes. The heavy equipment industry has tried to become greener in recent years, in part because some critics question their role in "reshaping," for lack of a better word, the environment.

Construction equipment manufacturers have dramatically reduced emissions, although they haven't had a choice as governments have tightened the standards.

Case decided to do something above and beyond, and found its cause in the form of "Dire States: The Drive to Revive America's Failing Infrastructure."

This is a program developed by Case and featured prominently on its website. Dire States has its own site, too, and a very sophisticated campaign as well.

Dire States "energizes the conversation" about the failing U.S. infrastructure. If you read the backstory

– wow, there are some problems that have a significant impact on the U.S. economy. They include crumbling roads, waterways, railways, ports, dams – you name it.

Case highlighted the problem by having an author/journalist named Dan McNichol drive around the country in a 1949 Hudson. The car was built the same year as most of the failing pieces of the infrastructure. Of course, the Hudson broke down along the drive across the U.S., as you would expect from something built in 1949, which is exactly the point Case was making.

McNichol did all sorts of promotion during his trip through all sorts of platforms. He and the Hudson – the car's name is Mrs. Martin, named after the sole previous owner – became celebrities in at least some corners of the world.

After the road trip, Case held a press conference at the world's largest construction show, CONEXPO, in Las Vegas. McNichol was there, as was Mrs. Martin. Case also brought in legislators and other key officials and had a very engaging conversation.

All this took place at the Case booth, by the way. Mrs. Martin was an attention grabber, looking old and weary, but cool nonetheless. She definitely stood out among the thousands of pieces of shiny construction equipment.

Many who passed by asked about her, giving Case an opportunity to tell its story – while positioning the company as an industry leader and an organization with a heart and a soul.

A few additional comments about Dire States:

- Case had high-level leaders on board. Some served as spokespeople and participated in events. Their support trickled down to all levels.

- Case told its story, too. The Starbucks and Case examples show the importance of telling your story. There is a chapter devoted to that very topic, but it's still worth noting that the companies had to tell their story to make the connections.

- Whatever the motive, the result is positive. Does Case care about the infrastructure? Without a doubt. Will it benefit by selling equipment if extensive infrastructure repairs are undertaken? Without a doubt. Which matters more to Case? I would answer that with a question of my own. Who cares? It's another win-win, and the world is a beautiful place when that happens.

Overall, a great example of a company finding a creative yet relevant cause to support and connecting with customers in the process – and, again, in an industry that is not considered on par with coffee houses in terms of social issues.

The pink room

At Marcus Hotels & Resorts, we have our own social causes and I'm proud to be part of one in particular.

A few of our associates came up with the "pink room" concept for the Intercontinental Hotel in Milwaukee.

The room has pink accents throughout as well as themed artwork. Guests who stay also can post a blog and do the writing from a pink laptop in the room. A portion of every pink room stay goes to an organization called ABCD: After Breast Cancer Diagnosis.

There are actually two pink rooms, and both are booked about 90 percent of the time. We've found that guests – many of whom have their own personal connections to breast cancer – find it rewarding to stay in the room because a portion of their hotel fees goes to ABCD.

The stays have made a difference. About $50,000 has been raised for ABCD in just a few years. Even better, ABCD has seen money beyond that $50,000, because guests also regularly donate to the organization while logged onto the pink computer in the room.

The pink room is Marcus Hotels & Resorts' TOMS Shoes story. People need to buy shoes, so they figure, "Why not do something good in the process?" With the pink room, travelers have to stay somewhere. Why not do something good, too?

Here are a few parting thoughts on social causes, given my close and personal involvement.

- Having a social cause brings your staff together. It's a team-building exercise. It's a chance to work toward something that isn't work itself. It's fun, motivating and rewarding for everyone.

- Social causes let others be leaders. Associates came up with the pink room concept and pursued it with a passion.

- Enthusiasm for a social cause can became contagious at all levels of the organization.

- You can make the world a better place, even if there is a business angle.

The last point is my favorite.

CHAPTER SIX

TELL YOUR STORY

I have a friend who is a former newspaper editor. At one time his paper ran a featured called "Everyone Has a Story."

It was a simple concept: A reporter would find a random local person – on the street or in those days maybe in the phone book – interview him and tell his story.

Sometimes finding that narrative was easy. In the first few minutes, the subject might disclose that he was part of the D-Day invasion, for example.

Others were a little tougher to draw out. My friend told me about a stay-at-home mom who grew up and went to college in her hometown.

She met her boyfriend in high school, and they had two young children. She provided in-home childcare to help make ends meet.

As an afterthought, she said she taught yoga. She added that teaching yoga wasn't all that interesting, and it wasn't exactly a passion either. It was more of a necessity. She had learned it 10 years ago as part of her rehab from a car crash.

The reporter knew they finally were getting somewhere.

She continued. The crash had been bad. It had nearly claimed her life and led more than one doctor to say she would never walk again.

"It was one of the most inspiring stories I've heard or read," my friend told me.

What amazed him most was the woman's attitude. "She continued to insist there was nothing remarkable about her at all. She kept saying, 'I'm just a stay-at-home mom.' "

∗ ∗ ∗

It's the same with your brand or your business. Your story might be obvious, like the D-Day survivor. Or you might have to dig a bit deeper to realize how good your story is, like the stay-at-home mom.

But the story is there. Of that I have no doubt. And that story could be the difference between success and failure. This leads to a very easy, two-step process that will help your brand and business succeed.

1. Find your story.

2. Tell it.

Why does all this matter, and what does it have to do with Millennials?

Lots. Remember, Millennials go shopping with a purpose. If they visit your business or look at your brand, they're probably close to making a purchase.

They also are an emotional group. If you can make a connection while they're looking at your product or brand, you have a good chance of success.

That connection can be the difference. In fact, I've seen this firsthand with Middle Sister Wine, sold in many grocery stores.

The wine isn't anything special, and it isn't all that cheap either. But wow, does it sell.

Middle Sister Wine often has large displays, which include its story: that it supports social causes for women. I've watched women approach the display, do a double take, stop and read about the social causes … and grab a bottle of wine.

Lots and lots of women do this. And think about it: They went from almost walking past the product, to learning its story, to buying it – all because Middle Sister Wine told them who the company is and what they represent.

If there is a takeaway from this chapter, I hope it is this: The key to unlocking the hearts and minds of Millennials is to tell them who you are.

ONE. Find your story

Not sure you have a story? I guarantee you do. Here are a few ideas.

Tell them your value story. Millennial impulse buys are built around emotion. What can strike a stronger chord than providing a benefit the Millennial values? Will your service or product improve their quality of life? Will it improve them – make them smarter, make them look better, solve a problem? These stories are home runs. Be grateful if you have one, and for heaven's sake, tell it.

Look at your history. This is often the easiest place to start. The details of your history or brand might jump out in an obvious manner, like the D-Day veteran. Yet every successful business has an interesting story to tell, similar to what my newspaper friend observed.

A business simply can't be successful without doing something interesting. Who started it, and how did it grow?

Older businesses also have faced adversity, trials and tribulations. Tell that story. It shows your business can rise to the occasion, and acknowledging your company's struggles conveys a genuineness that connects with Millennials.

Recent history works too. Millennials want to buy Kate Spade bags because they know something about her, and they connect with her name. But she is hardly ancient history.

Tell them how you make the world a better place. We talked about the importance of the greater good in Chapter 5. Those connections matter, and many brands have them.

Where some fail is identifying those charitable efforts as an important story. Some businesses and brands think the efforts are diminished if they tell the world about them – that publicizing them somehow makes their efforts less noble.

Wrong. You're identifying a valuable cause, and in doing so are exposing all your customers and prospects to that issue. What charity would not want you to tell that story?

What about your employees? Are their backgrounds unique? What about their education? Is their expertise in itself a story?

Some companies have researchers with amazing academic accomplishments that bring credibility and value to their products and services. Patents are great stories and create an air of knowledge and expertise. If you have patents, you have stories.

Do your employees have a passion? Do some of them share an interest you could highlight? For example, do many volunteer at the local food pantry?

Telling that story helps promote your business, and also helps bring attention to your employees' passions. A true win-win.

Tell your building's story. The Millennial might be standing in that building, thinking about buying your product. Make a connection. What is the building's history? Tell it. Who built it, when, and what materials were used?

Dig deeper. What other buildings and businesses were on the block at that time? Are images available?

Connections, right here and right now, lead to sales.

Look at your products. Where are they built? How are they built? Who builds them? What makes them unique?

Clothing and apparel brands miss some great opportunities here. They could teach about the textiles – that they come from India, they're handmade, and here's the process they follow.

Maybe feature a picture of a loom, include an explanation of why the weaving process is the way it is, and explain the positive impact that using these handmade fabrics has on the local culture.

A critical thinker would see the story and understand the product is unique, is authentic and is "local" in our sense of the word. But that story has to be identified and shared to be effective. When it is, Millennials will pay for that product.

Who is building the product? People identify with other people. That's why the broadcasters of the Olympics spend more time showing lifestyle features than actual events.

The Millennial is more likely to feel a bond with a particular person and his or her story – the woman operating the loom in India, for example. The weaver's story becomes part of your brand's story.

Look around the area. Bring local flavor into your establishment. Using local materials and telling their story is a possibility. For example, if your business conducts customer transactions over a counter, use quartz that is only available from a local quarry to top the counter. Then tell your customers about it.

This "local" concept is another area of great potential for retail and apparel stores, particularly the national chains. Local flavor would make each store unique and therefore connect in a way that seems to be lacking now.

For example, many historical buildings in Milwaukee have Cream City brick – old, really cool-looking materials. Having a modern store with a small section built of Cream City brick would tie into the local community.

An explanation of the history of the brick – and the earlier referenced quartz counter – would be crucial as well. Tell the story.

Create a story. What if you have virtually no history, no fork in the road, no patents and no quartz? Or maybe you have bits and pieces but nothing all that great?

Then it's time to develop a story. Is there a place inside your facility where employees can be creative – where they can come up with new concepts and product ideas? Create the space, get them engaged and talk about their suggestions – and how those ideas were utilized.

Stories related to social causes can be created, too. Tell employees you will provide financial support to a cause of their choosing if they volunteer. Then tell the story.

Everyone wins.

TWO. Tell your story.

You've identified your story. Now you have to tell it. Here are some key considerations.

Take a narrative approach. Millennials tune out if they feel they're being lectured. That means no pretension and no preaching. A narrative approach can go a long way. Stories draw in Millennials and don't feel like an orchestrated learning experience.

Shorter is better. This is a generation that grew up reading Wikipedia, not volumes of biographies. You have limited time and space to tell your story, which is fine. If you're posting information next to Cream City brick, you don't have space for thousands of words anyway.

Good writing matters. You still have to get your message across in that limited space, so every word counts – and every word has to expedite that connection.

Tell the story in more than one place. The company history should be on the website and displayed at its headquarters and key locations. The same with brand stories featuring key ingredients and benefits. These stories should be highlighted on the website and at the point of purchase, if possible.

Have others lend a helping hand. I referenced Case Construction when discussing social causes. Case started a program called "Dire States," which draws attention to our nation's crumbling infrastructure.

Case has done a great job of telling this story on a website, at trade shows, and at other places and in other ways. One key effort was creating a panel of industry experts. The experts pushed the cause through their own means. This gave the "Dire States" program more legs than a single source, even one as large as Case, could provide.

Use a prop. Props draw attention and create connections to the words. If an ingredient is crucial in your product, display it when you can. If history is your story, have the founder's chair or the workbench where it all began exhibited in the lobby (and an image posted on the website).

With Millennials, you're dealing with the Restoration Hardware generation. Old machines, equipment, tools, fixtures – they all are connections to your company's past. Millennials like to know sources, so those artifacts connect with them.

Use images. Pictures give stories meaning and context. If you have shots of the old factory, post them. Vintage photos of employees at work add dimension to your story and convey that you've always been the source.

Use technology. Despite the importance of history and artifacts, you can't beat technology when telling the story. Technology is how this generation accesses information.

Offer your point-of-purchase information on-site, of course. But explain that more details are available online, so Millennials can pull out the sacred phone if they like.

That's only the start. Businesses need to realize that new concepts such as augmented reality are now making a difference in reaching this generation.

∗ ∗ ∗

So where does this leave you? What can you do today?

Identify your story, or begin to create one.

Start generating content, and tell your story to the rest of the world.

Your business and/or brand will absolutely need to develop content to succeed with the Millennial generation. Without that story – whether it's based around value, history or something else – products and services are faceless commodities.

Without the story, this generation simply isn't buying.

PRACTICING WHAT
WE PREACH

How we told the Pfister story

The Pfister Hotel is a Milwaukee landmark with an absolutely fascinating history.

Yet it's a history that was never told, at least in a comprehensive manner. We changed that with the publication of a coffee table book, "The History, Art & Imagery of the Pfister Hotel."

It was quite the undertaking at 280-plus pages and hundreds of photographs. It also was an unqualified success, winning several prestigious awards and drawing considerable attention to the hotel. The book has been placed in libraries across the country, and someone seeking more information about the book, which was published in December 2013, contacts me at least weekly.

We didn't stop at the book. We created a high-end, documentary as well. It is posted on several websites and is shown on the in-room cinamas of the hotel.

The reason for the book and video, at the most basic level, was to tell the story of our landmark hotel, which opened in 1893. We knew it was a good story, but the deeper we dug, the more amazing it became. Before we were done, we had learned or confirmed that:

- Every president since William McKinley, who took office in 1897, has stayed at the hotel.

- President Kennedy kicked off his 1960 presidential campaign at the hotel.

- Elvis Presley stayed at the Pfister, as have hundreds of Hollywood celebrities.

- The hotel's Victorian art collection was unknowingly worth more than the hotel itself when the building was purchased by the Marcus family in 1962.

- The front of the building is in a unique location by today's design standards, because it originally was built for a horse and buggy turnaround when it opened.

- The Pfister was the first commercial building in the state of Wisconsin to have electricity.

- It was the world's first hotel to have individual thermostat controls in each room. (SC Johnson, the company that built the thermostats, was next door to the Pfister at the time.)

Pretty fascinating stuff. Yet not all was known until we really dug into the archives and searched other historical documents. Perhaps your business or brand has a more interesting history than you know.

A few other thoughts:

1. I typically preach brevity, and the book certainly is not brief. There is always a time for working outside the normal parameters. In this case, we had an abundance of history,

photographs and artwork that created impact. Common sense dictated that we share as much as possible.

2. The book also had enough of a "wow" factor that we were able to send out press releases, which led to positive press about the book. That carried the story even further.

3. The book won prestigious awards, including those associated with the 2014 International Book Awards and the National Indie Excellence® Book Awards. The honors gave the story longer legs and, once again, inspired others to tell our story for us.

4. While capturing interviews and creating this book, we realized we had the makings of an

interesting documentary (120 years of existence will do that). The documentary, which includes interviews with key figures as well as archive photos, won an award in the 35th Annual Telly Awards and a prestigeous Emmy nomination.

5. We will repurpose the content even further to reach Millennials. Specifically, we developed an augmented reality tour of the hotel. Thanks to that new technology, visitors can wear special glasses or use their smartphones to view content as they conduct a self-guided tour of the hotel and its historic spaces.

My own experience

I also would like to share a few words of advice.
As the project originator and coordinator, I saw
all aspects – writing, editing, printing, design,
distribution, press releases, you name it. Here are a
few lessons learned:

Sometimes you have to go for it. We were
all-in when developing the book. We utilized
talented photographers, editors, writers,
designers, historians and many others. We also
had a photographer spend two weeks straight –
day and night – to capture images of the hotel
at all times.

You need buy in. You need support to see the
project through. Telling your story on a grand scale

requires support at a fairly high level. Make sure you have that buy-in before you get the ball rolling too quickly.

You might be able to do it a lower cost than you think. I believe in paying for quality work, and we certainly did that with the book. We also found ways to reduce costs. For example, some historian helped at no cost because they wre presumably interested in the project.

All is well if you do it right. Once the book came out the questions ended. The quality of the product made it worth the time and money.

The book and video have been worth the effort, and many times over. That content is proof that if you tell your story – and tell it the right way – the public will listen, and your brand and business will benefit.

LEGO Movie is storytelling at its best

Whether it was Warner Bros. intent to tell a brand story when it produced "The LEGO Movie" isn't important. The blockbuster film is an awesome example of storytelling that resonates with both children and adults alike.

Like many successful companies (think Coca-Cola and Harley-Davidson), LEGO isn't promoting a product. It's selling something more, something intangible. Coke sells happiness. Harley sells a lifestyle. And LEGO? It sells possibilities.

The movie, made entirely with LEGO toys, follows the journey of an ordinary LEGO mini-figure who is thrust into the role of hero. To save his world (and get the girl,) he must prevent an evil leader from gluing the universe together.

While on his quest, the hero learns to believe in himself and the importance of working together. He also realizes that while following directions is good, using one's imagination can open up a world of new possibilities.

Told with humor and featuring catchy music, the story is a 100-minute ad for LEGO that never feels like it's selling something. Now that's creative storytelling.

CHAPTER SEVEN

SATISFY THE LOCAVORES

I knew we were onto something when diners at one of our Milwaukee restaurants started asking for a "local" lobster.

For the geographically challenged out there, Milwaukee is in the state of Wisconsin, and the state of Wisconsin is about a thousand miles from the nearest lobster in its natural habitat.

The obvious conclusion would be to say there is no such thing as a "local" lobster in Milwaukee. But sometimes the obvious conclusion isn't the correct one.

That's the case with the lobsters. The word "local" has become blurred, at least in the eyes of Millennials. Asking for a local lobster in Milwaukee is perfectly appropriate these days, and we couldn't be happier.

What about your business or brand? Has it evolved to feature local products and services, even when they're thousands of miles away?

The beginnings

I bring up the local conversation because many Millennials are considered "locavores." Originally, this meant they preferred food from a local source. But the concept now goes well beyond food, and the local aspect well beyond the neighborhood.

It now means knowing sources and providing products and services unique to a location. If you present your business and/or brand as having these characteristics, you will go a long way toward winning Millennials.

It's easy to see how Millennials originally came to embrace locavore ideology, particularly when it focused on food.

- Food that has a known source seems healthier – like it might not have been processed as much as something that comes out of a Hormel plant.

- The food should be fresher, too, since it only came from 100 miles away. (Local was originally within 100 miles, then 300 miles, and now I'm thinking it might be time to remove the mileage altogether.)

- It's good for the local economy. Why not help farmer Smith, who might not be your neighbor but at least lives within a county or two?

- It cuts out the middleman. Food from the farmers market should in theory be cheaper because you're going from the field to the consumer.

Early adopters

It's hard to say who first spotted the locavore trend, but my money is on grocery store produce managers.

For years customers spent summer months wandering through stores and leaving with all the staples – except for vegetables. The shoppers then drove from the grocery store to a roadside stand or a farmers market and finished their shopping.

A produce manager once told me this drives grocery stores nuts. The reality is that the same farmers, or at least their neighbors, are often sources for grocery stores. That meant shoppers were literally going out of their way to purchase the same produce they had walked by earlier at the grocery store.

But those roadside stands and farmers markets sure seem fresh, don't they?

Grocery stores have fought back, to a certain extent. Some now have short biographies of farmers, with a photo, in the produce areas. They understand the need to make that local connection – and they're telling their story.

The stores also have extended this concept to their meat departments. The freezers still are filled with meats, but most also have a glass case so shoppers can point at a particular steak and say, "Give me that one."

It feels closer than grabbing the pre-wrapped steak, though in theory they're often from the same cow.

Your efforts

What can you do to reach Millennials with locavore attitudes?

Tell your local story. The grocery stories are a great example. Let the world know that what you have is local.

Feature local people. People often are what make products and services local. Let a local craftsman set up shop in your space – at little or no cost. Get some local blood in there to help make a connection.

Need an example? If I were a retailer such as Macy's, I would have a cobbler inside the store. The cobbler would have space at no charge, but I would get something in return.

First, the cobbler setup would be unique. Second, it would be specific to that location.

It would be local.

I also would tell the cobbler's story, with a biography posted nearby – whether he is a fourth-generation cobbler immigrant from Transylvania or an MIT graduate who couldn't stand to work for The Man. It wouldn't matter. The story would be told, and it would be interesting. How could a cobbler's career path not be?

Find local products to sell or items to feature. Retail establishments have it easy on this front – at least at first glance. Bring in the local products and you're making the connection, right?

Yet this is an issue for many major retailers. Sometimes they don't have processes for finding, purchasing, pricing and placing these goods on their shelves.

They should. They have a chance to differentiate themselves and connect with Millennials.

Every store is virtually the same without those local products. That creates a dull, cookie-cutter feel. It also removes motivation to visit a chain store in multiple locations.

Think about it: If you live in Chicago, would you shop at a Target while visiting Los Angeles?

Probably not, because it's the same experience. Local products could make it a different experience.

Knowing sources makes them local

Sometimes a product that isn't local can in fact become local, and therefore connect with Millennials.

I saw this firsthand at one of our restaurants, Mason Street Grill, adjacent to the historic Pfister Hotel.

Years ago, as Millennials grew into a key demographic for our hotels, we realized many customers were asking the same question: Where does your food come from?

We said a truck. Pretty easy answer. Where did they think it was coming from?

Well, it turns out truck was too easy of an answer. (You learned earlier in this chapter that the obvious answer isn't always correct. This is another example.)

The Millennials meant the source of the food, not how it was transported, who grew it or how it was raised.

"Source" is a significant concept here. And it's where Millennial marketing opportunities abound. The customers mostly wanted to know something about the guy who provided the steak. Knowledge about his business mattered. Where was it? What made his products better than others? Was it a good, clean operation?

His personal story mattered, too. Was he a third-generation rancher who let his herd graze openly and eat naturally?

So we connected the dots and realized: It's knowing who the source is. That's what they're really asking.

Sure enough, the more we started talking about our sources, the more the Millennial customers communicated with our brand and the more they knew our story.

To connect with Millennials, go to the sources. They all have a story – every single one.

Mason Street Grill

We took the example of "local" to the extreme with a lobster promotion at Mason Street Grill. Remember, our customer wanted a "local" lobster. The chef, Mark Weber, traveled from Milwaukee to Tampa Bay and met with the source: a fisherman who works in the Gulf of Mexico.

Mark went out on the boat, as did a film crew. He spent a few days working traps with the lobsterman and hand-picked a few winners (an apt description to all but the "winning" lobsters).

The lobsters were boxed and shipped directly to Mason Street Grill. We told our diners abour the process and they loved it: Hand-picked lobsters were delivered to Milwaukee within 24 hours of harvest . . . not making them "local."

By putting that film together, we showed customers we care about our food sources – and that we know those who provide them on a personal level. We drove home the "fresh" point, too.

When the promotion started almost everyone ordered a lobster – including diners who said they didn't particularly love seafood. But the video connected that source to their plate, so they gave it a try.

The lobsterman was the kickoff to a campaign called "Straight to Your Plate," and many other stories followed. We created a website and continue to promote it on the menus. Diners access the website while at the restaurant. Had you any doubt a Millennial would pull out that phone and go online while sitting at his table?

The site has a few words and some videos – though nothing extremely polished, which is the plan. You can see people working in the background, and hear pots and pans clanging around. That's a good thing. It's "authentic," and of course Millennials love that.

The videos are about the content. These people – the sources of the food, if you will – tell their stories. They're fascinating. Millennials want to be informed, so inform them.

One woman owns a business named Purple Door Ice Cream, which we serve at Mason Street Grill.

Ice cream is this woman's passion. She dreamed of owning an ice cream parlor since she was in middle school. She discussed this with her husband – on their first date.

The video includes references to all the local products and ingredients she uses, and the positive impact those purchases have on the community.

Then we connect Purple Door Ice Cream with our brand through a second video. It includes a short conversation between the ice cream parlor owner and a Mason Street Grill chef. The chef then shows viewers how he is using the ice cream in his special waffles. It's sort of like a one-minute cooking show.

The reaction has been amazing. I bet 99 percent of the people who watch that video order the ice cream. The woman is local, she is authentic, she has a passion – she has a story.

This isn't about selling a scoop of ice cream or a free-range pork chop. It's about showing that we're connected locally. Even the locals we're connected to are connected locally. The tentacles are far-reaching.

More than food

The locavore concept started with food, but that doesn't mean it can't expand to other products and services.

In the hotel industry, boutique hotels are often considered local because they are one of a kind. They exist only in that one spot, and Millennials are more inclined to want to experience that.

Chains are now creating boutique experiences. Doing so successfully requires a lot of effort and attention to detail – local detail.

Boutique hotel guests want to wake up knowing they're somewhere different. Artwork helps on this front. Room art with images of Fisherman's Wharf or the Golden Gate Bridge are obvious examples that scream "San Francisco."

The larger point is that design and decoration bring in localization. In Texas, where everything is bigger, have a large, worn, leather couch in the lobby. In guest rooms, hang scenic photos or paintings by local artists, such as a rustic fence line cutting through a field of bluebonnets – the state flower. Or accent one wall in a full mural depicting a city scene or lifestyle image.

And then, at the restaurant, serve a local lobster.

Can't get fresher

Fans of local produce served as fresh as can be swoon over the Living Salad at the Blue Dragon Restaurant on the Big Island of Hawaii.

This unusual salad is presented in a small wooden planter where the mixture of delicate greens, grown from seeds, is accompanied by small scissors for harvesting, a selection of baby heirloom veggies and a spray bottle of vinaigrette to dress the medley.

Noah Hester, the restaurant's chef, likes the hands-on nature of the salad, which encourages people to make a connection with the source of their food.

Hester, who hopes to make the Living Salad its house salad, has served similar salads in a larger scale at catered events. Guests are delightfully surprised when the gorgeous green table centerpiece becomes a delicious and nutritious salad.

Awesome area eats

Mobile apps help bring Millennials closer to the local food they enjoy. Among the apps that help achieve this mission are:

- **Locavore:** This free app for iPhone, iPod touch and iPad, powered by Local Dirt, makes it a cinch to locate, purchase and cook nourishing foods that are organic, in season and grown on local farms.

- **Harvest:** Priced at $1.99, this app for iPhone, iPod touch and iPad offers helpful tips and photos for recognizing the fruits and vegetables that are fresh, ripe and in season. It also provides suggestions for storing produce for maximum flavor and longevity.

CHAPTER EIGHT

BE CONVENIENT.
OR BE LEFT BEHIND.

I had some time to kill during a recent visit to Los Angeles, so I strolled through the downtown area before eventually coming across the headquarters of the Los Angeles Public Library. I went inside – and freely admit that the promise of air conditioning played a significant role.

The building is massive, and I wondered how in the world someone would find a specific book in all that space – a single needle in that multi-story haystack. Pretty overwhelming.

At least it could have been. But just after my jaw dropped at the size of the place, I saw a sign for the "popular" section. It was right there, near the entrance.

It had every best-selling book and lots of popular videos. It was a library within the library.

I browsed other areas of the building, and the "popular" section was by far the busiest – even though it was definitely not the biggest.

Yep, the L.A. Public Library gets it. The staff realizes the public wants convenience and, in fact, is happiest when choices are narrowed.

Millennials take this to another degree: You absolutely must provide convenience. And if you don't narrow their choices, they're likely to narrow you.

Delivering convenience

Research shows Millennials demand convenience. They even love convenience stores. They are much more likely to get their toiletries from Walgreens than a Walmart SuperCenter. The value of convenience outweighs the cost.

How do you deliver that convenience? By putting your brand, products and services in front of them in creative ways. Then you narrow their choices and ultimately give the brick-and-mortar experience an online feel.

Narrow their choices

The big retailers are starting to understand this. Target is a good example, having launched TargetExpress stores, which are 20,000 square feet – about the size of a Walgreens or CVS.

The TargetExpress merchandise consists of many products found at the local pharmacy, but goes beyond that, too. Technological items are for sale – another nod to Millennials. The prototypes also have clothing affiliated with nearby colleges, creating at least a little bit of a local flavor.

Wal-Mart has its own down-sizing efforts under way on several fronts. It seems the giants realize that a huge selection is often too much for Millennials.

The downsizing is part of an overall trend to narrow choices, which research indicates is exactly what Millennials want. Too many options frustrate them and will lead them to look elsewhere.

Of course if you're offering fewer choices, what you have better be good. Make sure your research is thorough and up to date. You don't need to be a Wharton grad to know that fewer choices, all bad, are not what we're going for here.

If the narrowing is done properly, it will actually be a selling point. That's how I feel about buying suits from Express. The narrowing process doesn't help turn my visit into a transaction. That process is the reason I visit the store.

Express has two styles of men's suits – the photographer and the producer – and a few versions and colors within those styles. The suits are fashionable and contemporary, so I know I can't go wrong if I buy one.

Every other month, Express adds a few suits to the lineup – and that's it. (The "old" can still be accessed online.) Shirts are the same way, and there are plenty of socks to match the shirts.

It's a simple, easy concept that narrows choices, puts the right products front and center and makes the entire shopping experience intuitive and hassle-free.

Express actually helps me stay current, and it keeps me shopping on a regular schedule; every other month I pick up a suit and some shirts.

The website has more options, but presents them in such a fashion that you're not clicking your life away.

Make it feel like an online experience

The crammed retail rack is a swing and a miss with Millennials, who do not have the patience to review the volume of materials. Businesses do best with Millennials when they give their physical space more of an online look.

How can this be accomplished?

Create a filter in your store. Fewer choices, sorted neatly, connect with Millennials – almost as if a filter had been turned on in the store.

The shoe retailer ALDO is a good example of a business that understands this concept. ALDO focuses on shoes – mostly black shoes. Its stores are less than 200 square feet, with items displayed in an attractive fashion that mall passersby can easily see from outside the store. ALDO's products can be reviewed in a few minutes, because the choices have been narrowed for the customer.

Think of the shopping process at ALDO: The shopper enters and heads to the men's side of the store. Half of the store has been "filtered," if you will.

The shopper sees a shelf that holds shoes that are at least close to what he wants with business shoes on the left and casual on the right. He then looks closer for the perfect shoe, for colors (black or brown) and fine details. Then he asks for his size, purchases the pair and is out the door.

The process means the ALDO customer uses the store's layout and display almost like a website filter: Visit home page, click on "men's" shoes, click on a shoe, then further refine, add to cart, then check out.

Know that visibility matters. Key to the in-store experience is the presentation. The ALDO shopper can actually see the shoes; the shelves aren't crowded.

Remember TargetExpress? One of its design features is lower shelves, so customers can see throughout the store and easily locate what they want.

Visibility is how Millennials narrow their choices and navigate around physical locations.

Learn how others are working online. Most consumers regularly visit sites like Pinterest and Amazon, so they now are programmed to browse in a formulaic fashion. They tend to carry those tendencies to brick-and-mortar stores.

Understand what online processes are being implemented by the biggest retailers and social media outlets, and determine how to incorporate those into your operations as well.

Marry your online and traditional methods.

TargetExpress is doing this well. iPads are located throughout the store for customers who can't find what they need in the building. The iPads access the Target site, and orders can be made right then and there.

Most Millennials, of course, have their phones, but the iPads' presence is a convenience. The devices load to the Target page, and if there are questions, an associate is there to answer them. And, ultimately, the iPads' larger size means they are easier to use than phones and provide yet another added convenience.

From the store's standpoint, the iPads ensure the consumer makes the transaction now.

Let them customize like they're online. Some businesses provide the raw product and then offer consumers the ability to customize it, rather than putting every shape, size and color on the rack.

The Converse store in San Francisco is an example. It offers on-site silk screening, allowing shoppers to customize their Chuck Taylors. Customers use iPads to view a library of designs. This approach again helps shoppers work in a more "filtered" approach: Browse through the images, choose a design, then select a shoe. It works better than going through many colors and sizes multiplied by the 150 images.

Other convenient thoughts

A few final thoughts on how to provide Millennials with conveniences that could give your business a boost:

Change your selling process. Apple stores feature ambassadors who are there to help narrow choices for shoppers. This removes barriers and also makes the process easy for shoppers.

Package convenience with your products. A dash of convenience can make a difference. For example, a Swedish company, Middagrsfrid, delivers recipes and ingredients to customers' homes. The company makes its money off the ingredients, of course, but obviously entices busy shoppers with the entire convenient package delivered right to their doorsteps.

Make it a subscription. Few things are easier to manage than a subscription. Consider ways to make your products or even services subscription based.

There are some creative options out there. Need an example? A company called Freshades helps those who frequently lose or break sunglasses – a group that includes most of us.

For $9 per month, Freshades sends each subscriber an economical, stylish pair of sunglasses. One should, in theory, never be without sunglasses again. And talk about narrowed choices: The sunglasses simply arrive in the mail.

Narrowing choices is among the most important conveniences a Millennial can be offered. Many organizations, from giant retailers such as Target and Wal-Mart to the Los Angeles Public Library, understand its importance.

All those people can't be wrong.

Narrowing the dreaded
car purchase

A Facebook app is helping narrow options for those
purchasing a vehicle.

The app, called the autoTRADER autoLYZER,
uses data from the user's Facebook profile to help
select a car. The data includes photos, friend
listings and recent posts and offers three vehicle
options. It then links to the selected vehicles on
autoTRADER.ca, making the experience even
more convenient.

CHAPTER NINE
DON'T DESIGN FOR YOU. DESIGN FOR THEM

I'm sure you're well aware of the adage, "You never get a second chance to make a first impression." Appearance is everything.

Young, aspiring professionals sometimes ask me for advice on how to land that first big job. So, of course, the conversation inevitably turns to appearance.

We talk about everything: piercings, suits and ties, tattoos, wrinkled clothing, hair, belts, socks and shoes (brown or black.) And that's just the start.

The question then becomes what "really matters" when it comes to appearance. The answer is obvious, and I'm sure you know it.

"It all matters," I say. There isn't a right and wrong look in a moral sense, but the job candidate's appearance says something about who he is, and who he wants to be.

"Your appearance represents you as a brand," I tell each of them.

My peers in other industries would likely agree with this assessment.

Yet businesses sometimes forget that the way they present themselves tells customers who they are.

Can you be trendy if your suit is out of date? Can you be creative if you wear black and white? Can you be innovative if you are well-groomed? Sure, but first impressions will already be made.

No, businesses don't decide whether to wear wingtips. But their look says whether they're organized, trendy, old school, unconventional, clean, sharp, out of touch, sloppy, old, tired or energetic.

They do this through design. Design is your business' look. It's the way you present your brand and it makes an impression – good or bad – on a customer.

Whether the impression is positive depends at least in part on the observer. If you're interviewing for a job at a Motorcycle Repair Shop, you might do well going sleeveless and showing off your latest ink enhancement.

Interviewing at IBM? I would suggest a different approach.

Millennials, too, have their own preferred looks. Businesses need to understand Millennial preferences in order to connect with them.

Here are some key tips on how to ensure your design strikes a chord with Millennials.

Make it authentic with "real" materials.

Starbucks has made a living out of connecting with Millennials, whether through music, technology, social causes or space programming.

Starbucks is always looking for the next "thing," which can be a product or a way to deliver that product. That delivery of course includes the Starbucks experience – the feel you get when you walk in the door.

As the stores are built and updated, they are more "real" than ever.

The newest stores feature a lot of genuine materials – wood, brick and stone – which are about as authentic as you can get. Those materials ring true with Millennials. They feel permanent or historic.

If Starbucks is doing it, you know it's the way to reach Millennials, the cornerstone of its business model.

Think Restoration Hardware. Authentic also means handcrafted, handmade, unique and re-using old materials.

Many Millennials turn yesterday's materials into today's art. They'll take a component from just about anything, and re-use it and display it. Gears from an old machine are one example. Others are film reels from the old movie days, an old cart as a coffee table.

Like most Millennial thinking, this re-use concept is intertwined with other touchpoints. The re-used materials often have a story behind them, which Millennials like. They convert the hardware into artwork, showcase the pieces in their homes and share the stories of how they acquired the hardware, its history and how they transformed it. It connects them to it.

From a business standpoint, this means being more of a curator than a retailer. The retail chain Restoration Hardware is an example. Much of its merchandise feels older and more genuine – almost recycled when compared with some of its competitors.

Create a "social zone." Floor layout is a design element and it, too, makes an impression. Café-inspired marketing is one way floor layout connects with Millennials.

Some retailers have partnered with chains such as Starbucks to catch shoppers near the exit and entrance. Those are not the cafés I'm talking about.

The Millennial-marketed café should be in the middle of the store where customers can sit and take in the brand. The more time coffee drinkers spend there, the better is it for the surrounding business and the more comfortable the customers feel with the brand.

This is the same premise as convenience stores making very little profit on gas, but selling it to attract consumers who buy other items.

Some smaller retailers have put small bars in areas such as the shoe department. When consumers take a break, they take in the brand.

Incorporate "stay" factors. Materials used in design make customers comfortable. Some of the best efforts involve leathers, woods, task lighting, irons, brick or rocks. Not all these elements need to be present, but they do create comfort zones.

Book shelves are a great example. Remember, when have you been rushed out of a library? Stacked books create a familiar look, and their scent is a comforting reminder of the past.

Some design might look good initially, but its ultimate message may invite Millennials to leave.

For example, a hard-surface top, such as quartz or marble, can be a Millennial turnoff. The surfaces feel cold to the touch and make customers' laptops feel cold, too. The hard materials also are unforgiving and distracting while typing.

Does countertop material really matter? Absolutely. Uncomfortable people move somewhere else. It's a fact of life.

Wood is warmer and more forgiving, which is no doubt part of the reason Starbucks uses it.

Reflective materials also are an issue. Glare off the floor and table surface can make it hard to work on a laptop.

The hotel and tavern industries usually lead on the "stay factor" front. Bars often aren't bright; if you want people to look better – and thinner – turn the lights down. If you want them to look sexy, flicker the light. (Fire or candle).

Creating "stay value" also can be offering an incentive, or even signaling through a giveaway that the customer is welcome to stick around.

Lighting is so important, and it's often missed as a design touchpoint. Thanks to energy saving fanatics, LEDs and compact fluorescents are overused. They are put in places they shouldn't be: in an 85-year-old chandelier, in a lamp on a desk or over a dining table. The light from these sources is too white. Using an element or Edison bulb creates a warmer, amber glow, which customers find much more comfortable. (Even unconciously).

Design your website properly. Design doesn't just apply to physical locations. Websites, too, must connect and flow.

First, they must be uncluttered so shoppers can find what they want. They also can't be clunky. Smooth navigation is required, as Millennials (and all consumers) will become frustrated and likely give up if they can't quickly negotiate the site.

Websites have to be responsive. That means building a site so that no matter how it is accessed – through a phone, iPad, laptop or another device – it displays in an intuitive, reader-friendly format.

Make it unique. Authentic also means an individual creation, not another cookie cutter store. Most major retailers fall short in this area. You get the same experience no matter where the store is – New York, LA, Chicago, Omaha.

Some stores have figured this out. Whole Foods, Trader Joe's and Sendik's don't follow the one-look-fits-all approach. Local products are often incorporated, which of course make each store look different.

Millennials don't know exactly what they'll see when they walk in. That's why they might actually walk in.

Reinvent. Places can become too familiar and lose their appeal. Consider reinventing yourself to connect with Millennials. Doing so makes your brand relevant to newcomers.

Many independent restaurateurs like to change every seven years – the design, the name, the menu, everything – to create a reason to revisit and attract those who like to try something new.

So even if you did a complete makeover of your business, ask yourself, "How often are customers taking out their smartphones to share this experience with someone else?" If the sharing has died down, it might be time to reinvent ... again.

Your business has a look, whether you know it or not. Make sure it represents your brand properly – and you're not ink-covered at IBM.

Bridge to another business

The Aksel Paris store in the SoHo district of Lower Manhattan has a dual-purpose design. The store sells men's custom suits and shirts during the day and is an art gallery in the evening.

The modular nature of the store provides managers with the ability to redesign the space however they wish.

Hybrid work spaces like bike shop cafes have become common in today's retail market. However, modular fashion mixed with an art gallery space is a novel combination.

This spontaneity is just one interesting example of how businesses can utilize design and workspace.

A truly Millennial
Starbucks experience

All Starbucks are not built the same. That immediately becomes apparent during a visit to the store at Oak and Rush streets in downtown Chicago.

The store's design and other efforts are all about Millennials. You literally cannot turn your head without thinking, "They're doing that to reach Millennials."

- There are beautiful long, lumber bars. Each bar is from a single tree. The outside edges have not been cut straight but retain their original shape. They look very cool.

- The floors are simple concrete, the ceilings made of wood. Skylights illuminate the room.

- On one wall is an engineering-type drawing of how a coffee machine works – a nod to the Millennial love of components and origin.

- Signs in the store "tell the story" – for example, that the wall is made of brick rescued from other demolition sites. Beans are displayed, and their story told.

- Despite being part of a chain, the store is "local," with signs talking about the neighborhood. Canisters on display each have a letter and together spell out "OAK N RUSH," the store's location.

- Stay factors are at work, too. Patrons relax on leather seating and work at wooden tables.

Speaking of stay factors, the store serves alcohol after 2 p.m.

- Authentic touches are everywhere. Split wood, like that ready for a campfire, is stacked along one wall, near an old milk can.

You know what else? The store is crowded – all the time.

CHAPTER TEN

DON'T BUILD IT FOR YOU.
BUILD IT FOR THEM.

It's rare to have an opportunity to start from scratch – to build something the way we want, from the very start. That's the case for most of us both personally and professionally.

Think about it. We overlook imperfections when we buy homes. In our professional lives we adjust, tweak and improve plans and strategies. We "make the best of it." And we should, as that's often what the job requires. Seldom do we have the luxury of making something exactly the way we want it.

But what if we had a chance to start from scratch – to build something precisely the way we wanted? What if we could create the perfect independent hotel that can uniquely cater to the need of today's traveler? The traveler from the largest travel demographic ever.

This new brand will be specifically designed to capture Millennials from the time they find us on the internet – or better yet, hear about us from a friend before they even begin that online search. We will use what we know about Millennials – much of which has been shared in this book – to make sure the experience is positive and engaging from start to finish.

Here are key characteristics of that built-from-scratch boutique hotel. And don't forget: Among these characteristics are lessons that can be applied to your business, as the travel industry represents a leading indicator of buying habits and trends in connected consumerism.

Small and agile. The larger hotel brands are aircraft carriers. They are s-l-o-w to react to a changing marketplace and to recognize and correct mistakes. Often, the big brands churn out "new" ideas, that are already in the market by the time they are implemented.

Our hotel will be responsive, in part because of the size: 200 or fewer rooms compared with the 800 to 1,000 rooms at the major brands, which need large conventions to survive.

Those bigger brands mandate changes from on high, often from a location hundreds or even thousands of miles away. Our hotel will make local decisions based on input from our guests and frontline staff, and the ideas will be implemented immediately.

Customer service. It will be exceptional. We will hire associates who feel passionately about providing it and will maintain that focus at every level. Hiring will be based on attitude, not necessarily skill. Let's face it: We are offering an experience, not performing brain surgery.

Convenience. Our booking system will be smartphone friendly, as that is increasingly the tool Millennials use. The process will be smooth and seamless with a booking taking no more than four minutes. Yes, there is an app for that.

An app that features mobile check-in and check-out can shorten that time, and also include customer preferences. We'll provide convenience and customer service.

A local feel. Local ties are important to Millennials. Remember all the "locavore" talk in Chapter 7? Our hotel will be local.

- We will feature food and drink from local sources and tie our hotel into the surrounding neighborhood and city through design and by telling our story.

- We will be local because locals will be running our hotel. We will fill our facility with people who live down the block – or at least in the same city. This will be accomplished by creating a bar and restaurant so engaging and appealing they draw guests from near and far. We will target locals, not hotel guests.

- The size of the hotel will feel intimate and part of the neighborhood. Large groups cannot be accommodated in a hotel with 200 rooms. That's a good thing. There won't be hundreds of name-tag-wearing guests, registration desks or banners in our lobby. Multiple, smaller groups create diversity – and that diversity in turn creates a local feel. Just lots of people from different places, some farther away than others, hanging out. Guests may assume the guy next to them is a local.

Be on many shelves. Being found is really about being "on every shelf," so to speak. If a company were in a retail setting, it would want products in many locations to increase the likelihood a customer would spot its brand. In other words, it would want its product on many shelves.

It's the same with a hotel, though our products are on virtual shelves.

One shelf is simply the internet – and, specifically, generating high placement during searches. We accomplish this through Search Engine Optimization, which will benefit from:

- Our connection to social media.

- Our commitment to tell our story.

- Our desire to make guests ambassadors and have them tell our story, too, across other channels.

The initial discovery on the internet "shelf" is only the start. We need the visitor to click to our site – to pull the product from the shelf and give it a closer look.

That click will bring visitors to an organized, appealing, easy-to-navigate (and interface with) website. Its design will be responsive so it recognizes the device being used to access it (smartphone, tablet, laptop.) That recognition leads to a more informative and user-friendly experience.

Another "shelf" is provided by travel sites such as Expedia and Travelocity. While I don't love the fees these sites collect, I do want the exposure they provide and am willing to pay for it. We need to have our product on many online travel sites.

It's up to us to limit the cost of the product placement. Ultimately, if we do it right, we can have the best of both worlds – we can be on the shelf and avoid the fees.

How? First, many users visit these sites as the first stage of their research. They start with, say, Expedia, then go to Travelocity, then TripAdvisor. They read the consumer comments and then go to the hotel's site for more information or to compare prices.
If the prices are the same, they usually will book directly with the hotel. If this occurs, we gather the customers' preferences to use again and attain the guest at a lower cost, though we did benefit from their customer reach (shelf) and we converted them on our brand site.

Therefore, we must make our online prices at least equal, whenever possible, to the travel sites. But more times than not, providing a unique offering or greater value proposition will be the key.

We'll still lose some guests who book through those sites. It's simply math; we can't win them all. But when those guests check in, we'll encourage them to work directly with us next time.

"I see you used X.com to book your reservation. That's great, but we do offer complimentary parking for those guests who book directly with us. Maybe next time you'd like to consider that route. Here is a card with our website and 800 number."

Those customers who booked directly with us online will be positively rewarded to reinforce that behavior. "I see you booked through our site, and as a reward, we would like to provide you with free parking," a free amenity, a complimentary drink or something along those lines.

Last but not least, all customer reviews – good or bad – will be on industry sites such as Trip Advisor. We will take steps to ensure there are reviews, perhaps offering an incentive to in-house guests who complete a survey or write a review during their stay or upon departure. Reviews do more than inspire peers. They also help search engines find us.

Help travel agencies help their customers.
Millennials seek adventure whether traveling for personal or professional reasons, and often rely on travel agents to guide them. Travel agencies are in fact another shelf.

We will need to ensure travel agents are aware of our hotel – that it's local, that it can be an adventure, and that it will provide their customers with an outstanding experience. We

will make the travel agents look good by giving
their clients the experience they want.

We will push our story out to travel agencies. Doing
so will make their jobs easier, as Millennial travelers
often ask them for advice. "What's a cool hotel in
Chicago? Where should I stay if I'm in Dallas?"

We will have answers for the agents. We will
describe the experience we provide and the agents,
in turn, will tell it to their customers. If we have
something specific or unique – a story – it will
make the agent appear to be on the inside track.

Providing this information has become
increasingly important since the proliferation
of online travel sites, which have been direct
competition to those working offline. The travel

agents have to be a more valuable resource than the internet, and telling them our story helps them bring more value to their customers.

Just being able to tell their customers a few words about a specific hotel can make a difference. "They have a fantastic rooftop bar. You have to take your client there." Or, "This is Eddy Vedder's favorite hotel when he's in town."

We will help the travel agents be ambassadors of our product.

Tell our story and help others tell it, too. We will need to do a great job telling our story. That will start with our website, which will feature engaging and interesting content that positions us as a local, unique hotel.

When applicable, we will discuss the history of the building and the neighborhood on our hotel's website. We will share details about the bar and restaurant as well as the sources of our food and drinks.

Our website will feature images taken by professional photographers and links to customer photos on sites like Flickr. The travel sites use these photos on their pages, so the images reach beyond those who visit our site. Quality photos help both us and our ambassadors tell our story. The photos are present on multiple shelves.

We will be engaged in social media, as guests want to connect with us and tell their stories about staying with us.

- Our hotel will need to be adventurous enough that Millennials will want to announce their presence using tools such as Foursquare, Instagram and Snapchat.

- We will have a Flickr and Pinterest page where guests can post photos of their stay. The photos will capture guests in candid moments, enjoying the hotel's amenities. These will have a powerful, personal connection to our guests' followers, who also are our prospects.

- We will need to be present on other social media – Facebook, Instagram and more as they develop – because Millennials are likely to find us this way and because they enable the all-important peer endorsements.

A grand entrance. If possible we will create a showcase piece that will all but force Millennials to share their story.

For example, an enormous statue of David stands in front of a hotel in Louisville called 21C Museum Hotel. How impressive is the sight? Next to 21C is the Louisville Slugger Museum & Factory. Yet more people take and post a photo of themselves in front of David than the large baseball bat in front of the museum.

That means photos of David – and 21C's guests – are on Instagram, Facebook, Twitter, Flickr and every site you can think of. The photos are of people smiling, laughing and having a good time at 21C. They look authentic, too – real people having fun.

Each photo is a highly valued peer endorsement. In this case, a picture is worth a thousand ads.

Activity in the lobby. Millennials want immediate gratification when they walk through the door. They want instant acknowledgement that choosing the hotel was the right decision.

Our lobby will need to make that statement. There will be activity and energy. There will be diverse groups represented, so the Millennial sees, "There are people like me here."

We drive activity by making the lobby the building's only common area, often commingling the bar and restaurant. This ensures activity isn't diluted to other areas.

"Stay factors" will be incorporated, including authentic materials, and some form of fire (fireplace, candles, special lighting) as well. The designincludes water, proper lighting and fire scenography done the right way.

A bar and restaurant that can stand on their own. Major brands struggle with developing a bar and restaurant that connect with individuals because they are so busy pleasing the masses.

Our restaurant and bar will feature unique food and drinks created by craftsmen. The themes will be enticing enough to draw in locals, our guests and guests of the huge hotels, who no doubt want to have some sort of experience outside the norm during their travels.

We will devote energy and money to the bar and restaurant because they are part of the hotel's identity. But the restaurant will be on its own to create appeal and demand in order to stay independent from the hotel. Locals will see it as a neighborhood restaurant.

There also will be local ties – for example, a drink that mimics a hometown celebrity's favorite, or food from a local source.

A hotel room that makes a difference, too. Many in the travel industry say you book the room because of the public space, including the look of the lobby. That might be true, but the room remains an essential component of the experience. The room also has to justify the cost.

To ensure the experience is exceptional, our rooms will have three zones: refresh, reprieve and relax.

Refresh. Guests encounter the "refresh" area when they walk into the room. It includes the bathroom and a closet. It will have as many features as possible to create somewhat of a spa feel, a needed transition at the end of a business meeting or a long day of travel.

Reprieve. The "reprieve" area is for resting. It is separate from the refreshing area; in fact, neither area is visible from the other. The reprieve area includes the bed and is the true core of what guests are paying for, or at least that traditionally was the case.

Relax. The relaxing space, the third component, utilizes a half-wall to create separation from the sleep space.

The relaxing space is a den-like structure with a comfortable couch, a great working desk and a television that can be utilized to review presentations or, of course, for more traditional viewing.

Separation is key. It's important for business travelers to have an area to relax that is not where they sleep. Rooms feel larger and guests feel more at home if they relax somewhere other than the bed.

We'll add a touch of inspiration as well. Either the reprieve or relax space will feature an element that can be shared with real-time users. It could be a compelling piece of art, an inspirational quote or a full wall mural that prompts guests to photograph and share it.

The room's design also will be authentic. It will utilize real materials, such as brick and wood, and incorporate local art.

✱✱✱

Many elements will come together at our hotel: Storytelling, design, scenography, "locavore," customer service, adventure … and no doubt more.

Great experiences result when these elements complement each other. And when we have great experiences, we want to share them.

Millennials are the cornerstone of the efforts surrounding our hotel. They want people to know where they are and what they're doing. These experiences are an extension of who they are, and they want to talk about them – now through social media as well as in the traditional sense.

You might say spreading the word is their voice. This place is the vision they might have that fits best with their own personalities and aspirations. Creating an environment so compelling that they want to share their story is our vision.

Customizing. Targeting. Improvising. Re-tooling. Staying focused and aware. These are tools that any business, in any industry, can use to better reach the Millennials.

CHAPTER ELEVEN

REACH THEM WITH TECHNOLOGY

The Pfister Hotel is loaded with history – and in all corners of the building, too.

I told some of those stories earlier in this book, but in a nutshell, the Pfister is the stopping spot of presidents and celebrities. It's an innovator, including the nation's first hotel to feature individual climate control in each room. And it's a monument to art, with a collection of Victorian work that would make Bruce Wayne weep tears of jealousy.

The story is great, to be sure. But how do you brag without boring? How do you tell such a great story to a generation that wants the information, but also doesn't like being lectured?

You tell the story on their terms. You create great content and then utilize technology to operate in the Millennials' realm.

One other thing: You put the story out there, but you let them find it on their own. Then it becomes their discovery instead of your lecture.

That's a great theory, but how is it accomplished?

Create great content. No matter what is used to deliver the content, the message still matters most. If you don't get the message right, you can't succeed further in the process.

In some ways, this reminds me of the old video days. Back in the 1980s – a few years before I opened my store – there was quite a public debate over whether Beta or VHS would be the format of choice. Around that same time, a similar shakeout occurred in the music world, where the decision was between 8-track and cassette players.

Even during those debates, content mattered the most. You bought a Beatles cassette because you liked the Beatles, not because you liked cassettes.

We have to remember that content always matters most. That's what the public sees. That's what has value. The way of delivering that content will change, but quality will withstand the test of time.

Don't forget: properly developed content can be adjusted for the ever-evolving world of technology.

Then find the technology. We've developed some quality content that will withstand the test of time. Now we need customers and prospects to take a look at it in the here and now.

This is where the delivery method does matter. If the Beatles' music is only on 8-track, and I have a cassette, there are going to be disincentives for me to buy that music – no matter how good it is. I might say to myself, "Led Zeppelin is pretty darn good and they're on cassette, so maybe I'll just pick that up instead."

You need to find technology that makes it more likely your great content will be found and embraced. What are some of those technologies? The first is an old Millennial favorite.

The smartphone. Just about everyone has one, right? Make your content accessible.

Specifically, we have a self-guided tour that enables Millennials to read pop-ups on their smartphones as they look at interesting art or hotel features. The content can start with an explanation of the art and a few words about the artist. We also developed related videos that can be displayed on smartphones, adding another layer of information.

The smartphone makes it easier for guests to access more resources than any wooden plaque ever could. That phone also is a social media tool, and we love how quick and handy it is for those on the tour to post our story for all the world to see.

If you think the smartphone tour sounds pretty cool, you'll love augmented reality.

Augmented reality (AR) is more interactive than the smartphone. More life-like too, and you can do more with it.

With AR, the participant puts on Google glasses, or uses their smartphones, to view full motion images based on where the person is looking.

How about an example? Let's say the Millennial looks up, toward the ceiling. A full motion video starts playing. The cherubs painted on the ceiling move in circles, and a narrator provides further background.

At the Pfister Hotel in Milwaukee, this is all ready happening with interesting features throughout the building and 80 pieces of artwork. The art, via video, will tell the story behind their work.

Of course the artists are actors who were shot in HD video – an obvious necessity given they lived during Victorian times. But the Pfister also has living artist residents who talk about their favorite pieces on video.

We're early adopters for several reasons. First, we want to reach Millennials, and this technology is a way to do so. We will not limit the tours to hotel guests. We are very much in favor of non-guests taking the tour. It's just more people helping us tell our story.

Our history is also one of innovation, and we want to maintain that. We will be the first hotel in the U.S. to offer an AR tour. Once again, we're leading the way.

We also like the technology because it links the old with the new. The technology makes us a little more modern, despite the age of some of the pieces we highlight.

It's also about self-discovery. Those on the tour can walk to pieces that interest them and access multi-

media – and multi-dimensional – resources to learn
more. Yet it's learning on their terms. They are
discovering as they move along.

∗∗∗

The process starts with good content that is worthy
of discovery – and in fact validates the searchers'
efforts when uncovered.

This content doesn't just have to be for self-guided
tours. It can be a restaurant posting reviews or
a menu to be seen by those who pass down the
street with the right app. It can be any business
creating content and telling its story.

Create quality content and post it on the best
technological fit you have right now. Keep your

eyes and mind open, and be ready to add or adjust technologies as needed.

Self-discovery takes it from there. No lectures, just content that can be found on the Millennials' terms. And they will look. Self-discovery is in their DNA.

So is talking about what they've found – in other words, telling our story.

Works for us.

Interesting uses of augmented reality

- Brick-and-mortar American Apparel stores
  are using augmented reality to give in-store
  shopping more of an online feel. American
  Apparel has an AR app, which provides a variety
  of information and options to in-store shoppers.
  Consumers are able to access customer reviews,
  view slide shows and change a product's color
  on their smartphones – all while standing in the
  physical store where they can try on clothes to
  make sure they fit.

- IKEA uses AR to help customers "place" furniture
  in their homes, at least in a virtual sense.

- TOPSHOP has launched an AR app, TOPSHOP
  Kinect, utilizing Microsoft's Xbox to take the
  fitting process to another level. The user poses with
  arms above his head and lets Kinect take a photo.

The viewer then motions to try on different styles,

colors, etc. The garment is placed over the body

as if it's a non-virtual experience.

CHAPTER TWELVE

FIND THEM ON THEIR SMARTPHONES

Pause and take a look around the next time you're in a coffee shop.

A few patrons will talk to each other. A few others might look at tablets or – gasp – a printed publication. Yes, they're still out there.

But most in that coffee shop will be doing something on their phones: texting, reading, researching or utilizing apps.

In fact, even those who are talking to others are probably glancing at their phones frequently. And those phones are never more than an arm's length away. For many, the smartphone has become an extra appendage.

Marketers to Millennials need to – dare I say it? – wake up and smell the coffee. That phone is everything.

The hard numbers

Research on Millennials and their smartphone use is revealing.

Nearly half of Millennials – specifically 48 percent – use a smartphone multiple times daily. But they don't use it to talk. The phone is the preferred method of communication to only one in four Millennials. They want quicker, less personal communication.

The phone means a lot to the Millennial, with 28 percent saying they would not surrender their smartphone in exchange for broadcast television.

The phone isn't the only tool. Millennials are significantly more likely than all adults to multiscreen, or access different types of technology at the same time.

The prevalence of the smartphone doesn't seem to translate into an online shopping preference. In fact, Millennials are no more likely to shop online than adults from other generations.

However, Millennials are more likely to use smartphones to redeem coupons. They also are more likely to be influenced by an online or a mobile ad.

How do you get that mobile number?

The fact that the smartphone is always at hand means you can reach them on it at any time.

That's the good news. The bad news: They don't like to give up their mobile numbers, with some research showing they consider these numbers as personal as their credit scores.

There are ways around that. Millennials spend much of their time engaging with social media, so marketers with a good presence in that arena can reach them on their smartphones without needing the actual mobile numbers.

How do you engage on social media? Through the same methods discussed earlier: Telling your story is one way, supporting a social cause is another. Behaving properly – in other words, not pestering – helps peers encourage others to connect with you on social media.

Here's another key point about mobile numbers: Millennials don't like to give up those numbers, but they sometimes will when offered appealing incentives.

In one study, 20 percent of Millennials who initially refused to provide a mobile number changed their minds in exchange for 10 percent off a purchase. The percentages still aren't great, but some mobile numbers are being surrendered.

What does this mean to your marketing efforts?

The hard numbers prove the importance of the smartphone. With that data in hand, marketers can take specific measures to promote their products, services and brand. Here are some key tips and observations:

The smartphone is a research tool that fits in a purse or pocket. Millennials will use their smartphones to learn about you, so be ready to impress them when they do.

- Utilize responsive web design so they can access your website from their smartphones. RWD creates a user-friendly interface that adjusts to whatever device is accessing the site. Millennials will quickly look elsewhere if they visit a site on their phones and have trouble navigating or even seeing the site.

- Make sure your most important content is prominent on the RWD version. That means social causes should be easily spotted, as well as links to social media and the peer endorsements that go with them.

- Quality images draw in web visitors. Be sure to have them and to display them properly to engage.

- Make your address easy to find. Millennials might just be visiting your page to put your address into a GPS. Don't overwhelm them with data at the expense of the one thing they really need.

- Make the transaction a click away. Navigating through multiple layers to make a purchase can be frustrating, particularly on a phone. Make the transaction process simple, and you'll reduce frustration and increase sales

They have their smartphones on at your place of business. You better believe they're checking you out, even while standing inside your business.

- They might be comparing prices, so ensure you are consistent in your brick-and-mortar and online locations.

- Millennials will stand inside your doors and check whether the guy down the road offers the same product or service at a lower cost. But remember: you can be priced higher and still win by providing great service and, of course, being more convenient – two key Millennial concerns.

- View the on-site research as an opportunity to connect with them while they're at your business. Close the deal by telling your story. Promote social causes online, too.

- Millennials like online coupons and special offers, which are another way to close the deal.

Papa Murphy's does a good job of this. The take-and-bake pizza maker invites website visitors to sign up to receive regular emails with exclusive offers and coupons.

But what if your customers are standing in your business and don't want to wait for weekly or monthly emailed coupons? They're hungry for instant gratification.

Follow Papa Murphy's example and give it to them. Reward them on the spot if they agree to receive occasional text messages from your company.

While waiting to order at a Papa Murphy's store, I saw signs promising a free item if I joined the company's text club. Curious to see how the program worked, I texted the keyword as directed by the sign.

By the time I reached the counter, I'd registered and received a message offering me free cookie dough with my purchase. The reward was worth surrendering my mobile number; since then, Papa Murphy's hasn't abused it by sending excessive texts. That kind of exchange is a sweet deal for customers and businesses alike.

- Along the same lines, offer immediate incentives for Millennials who connect with you on social media while at your business. For example, a discount or free drink for every customer who takes a photo at your business and posts it to Instagram. Or give an exclusive offer to customers who follow your business on Facebook. You can connect with them on their phone when they follow you on social media. You don't need that mobile number.

- Encourage them to use their cameras. Create a photo opportunity at your business. If you do, they'll snap the image and post it on social media.

Remember the statue of David in front of the 21C Museum Hotel in Louisville mentioned in Chapter 10? That's the kind of photo opportunity that's irresistible to Millennials.

LEGOLAND Discovery Center Chicago offers dozens of opportunities just like that. Sure, the center has a movie theater, some rides, plenty of stations where kids (and often their parents) build creations with LEGO bricks and several ramps where they race the custom LEGO vehicles they assemble.

But throughout the place, guests encounter life-size statues of kid-favorite characters made entirely of LEGO bricks, such as Harry Potter, Indiana Jones and Santa Claus.

"Who wants a picture taken with Darth Vader?" a mom asks her boys, who happen to be wearing Star Wars T-shirts. Other families wait their turns as the mom snaps a photo with her phone, then moves aside to post it on Facebook.

The mom's friends—many of whom have visited the Discovery Center with their own families—are reminded when they see that image on Facebook that it's been awhile since their last LEGOLAND visit. Maybe the sight of those smiling faces next to Darth triggers a memory of the fun their own kids had there and prompts them to plan another visit.

That's the power of photo opps. The Millennial with smartphone in hand is essentially bringing storytelling tools into your business. Take advantage of that.

Apps are your friend. Millennials are loyal and would be willing to download your app if they plan to do business with you again. Apps also make the buying process easy. Convenience matters to Millennials.

Scholastic Book Fairs could've written the book on simplifying customer purchases. It designed an app to help busy parents quickly find appropriate reading material for their children during school book fairs.

Scholastic holds more than 125,000 book sales at schools across the nation each year, which means a lot of parents are helping choose books for their kids.

But who has time to research the best books for a second- and fifth-grader before the event? Or to scan the back covers of hundreds of titles at a crowded book fair?

Enter the free Scholastic Book Fairs app. Downloading it makes it a snap to get just the information a parent needs. A quick scan with a smartphone of the cover or barcode of any book at a Scholastic sale brings up a story summary, the book's price, and its age, grade and reading levels. It even recommends books, so if your second-grader loved the Captain Underpants series, the app suggests similar books your child might like.

The app simplifies the selection process and helps parents make educated buying decisions on the spot.

- If you offer an app, prominently display it on your RWD site.

- Promote your app in your brick-and-mortar locations, too.

- Apps are an opportunity for you to push content out to the Millennials. Again, you'll have to find the balance between not enough and too much. But apps do enable communication without the need to acquire mobile numbers.

A few other smartphone notes ...

- Their smartphones are on while they're doing other stuff. Complimentary content can help connect. For example, social media – including Twitter – often are followed while Millennials are watching a television show or sporting event on another device.

- They use their smartphones as a GPS. That means you don't have to provide directions all over your website. But do post your address up high and visible on your site.

- Marketers have a tough task. Millennials don't like to be "harassed," yet in some cases respond when they are. Being offered an incentive to surrender a mobile number is one example. Another is social media advertising. Fewer than one in five Millennials likes advertising on social media sites or receiving promotional texts. Yet they are more likely than other adults to accept these techniques. Maybe the key is providing a message that has value or connects in some way.

***

The prominence of the smartphone frustrates some businesses. They find the constant price checking and researching to be distractions.

Are they right to feel that way? It doesn't matter. The smartphone, or other such devices, are here to stay. Marketers need to view them as what they are: tools essential to reaching customers.

CHAPTER THRITEEN

COME UP WITH YOUR PLAN

I've been to seminars with inspiring speakers and engaging panelists. Yet sometimes as I walked away my smile became a look of bewilderment as I pondered a very simple question.

Now what?

Hopefully you've put some of the "Now what?" pieces together as you've read this book. Some of you might have action plans already.

Perfect. I couldn't be happier.

For those of you who need a little homework to get the ball rolling, here are four key follow-up steps.

ONE. Make sure others "get it."

You probably understand the importance of Millennial marketing. After all, you are reading this.

Now you have to make certain others at your business have received the message so they, too, buy in.

Start by telling them Millennials will likely surpass the spending power of the boomers by as early as 2018. Then let them know that Millennials are expected to spend $1.7 trillion annually in the U.S. by 2020.

For more supporting information, go to the first chapter of this book, "Know Who They Are."

The point is that the numbers show the importance, and hopefully make a case as you pursue improvements at your business.

TWO. Start creating great content.

Understanding your story, and telling it, is crucial to Millennials.

But how do you start? Chapter 6 is entirely devoted to telling your story. Some quick advice would be to involve and assign fact-gathering missions at your business.

Learn the history of your business, or the source of materials. Where do your products come from? What makes them unique?

Make a commitment to developing exceptional content that can be the foundation of other efforts. Really good content can be sliced and diced and repackaged across many mediums and platforms.

Remember: Technology and the associated delivery methods will change, but the message will not.

Make a commitment to creating that solid content foundation and building off it.

THREE. Take a tour of your business.

Walk around your business with a fresh set of eyes. You know what connects with Millennials. How could your business do this better?

Do signs tell your story? Are materials authentic? Do newcomers feel welcome? Does your design encourage customers to stay?

Watch employees on your tour, too. Do they properly engage customers? Do they have the passion your business needs to reach the next level?

Don't limit the tour to your own observations. Have an outsider who is unfamiliar with your operation take a stroll with you. What do they notice? What jumps out at them?

Take a "tour" of your website as well. Is it welcoming? Easy to navigate? Convenient?

FOUR. Get started.

What's most important is getting started – somewhere, somehow – because this group needs to be reached. And they need to be reached now.

Not to go all "Poltergeist" on you, but "They're here."